www.pocketessentials.com

First published in Great Britain 2002 by

Pocket Essentials, P O Box 394, Harpenden, Herts, AL5 1XJ, UK

Distributed in the USA by Trafalgar Square Publishing, PO Box 257, Howe Hill

Road, North Pomfret, Vermont 05053

Copyright © Steven P McGiffen 2002

Series Editor: Paul Duncan

A CIP catalogue record for this book is available from the British Library.

ISBN 1-904048-16-1

2 4 6 8 10 9 7 5 3 1

Book typeset by Wordsmith Solutions Ltd

Printed and bound by Cox & Wyman

CONTENTS

CONTENTS

Introduction: Global Moments

'Another world is possible.'

Slogan of the World Social Forum

1 January 1994, Chiapas: Hundreds of peasants emerge from the forests of southern Mexico and declare themselves in revolt against the established order. Poorly armed but well-organised, they have been driven to revolt by inescapable poverty and are led by a colourful, quixotic figure whose precise political views are sometimes hard to pin down.

Peasant revolts have punctuated history. If you leave people with nothing to lose and no constitutional means to improve their situation they will eventually fight back. Some of these revolts will be well organised, others less so. Some will embrace authoritarian ideologies. Some will be anarchistic or libertarian in methods and goals. Some will enjoy a measure of success, while others will see their leaders co-opted by the status quo, their dedication to the people's interests diluted or forgotten. Still others will end in hails of bullets from ambushes or firing squads. Chiapas falls within these boundaries, recognisable as one more peasant revolt in the long history of such events. But Chiapas was also something else, something different. It was a global moment, the first revolt of the age of globalisation.

A number of elements made Chiapas into a curtain-raiser for a drama which would be played out everywhere over the next few years, and whose end we are very far from seeing. From the paddy fields of India to the streets of Seattle, globalisation has been answered by a resistance which is huge, broad and growing.

Why can Chiapas be seen as the cradle of this movement?

While the revolt had its roots in grievances going back to the first conquistadors, its immediate spark was provided by the North American Free Trade Agreement (NAFTA). And NAFTA is a small but important part of the phenomenon which has come to be called 'globalisation,' whose underlying process is 'liberalisation,' the removal of barriers to the movement of goods, finance and services.

The argument for free trade is simple and powerful. Protectionism, it says, doesn't work. Take the controversial decision taken by the United States in March 2002, to impose heavy tariffs on imported steel. The move came in response to pressure from powerful steel corporations, whose wealth buys influence in Washington, and their employees, whose votes are concentrated in a number of marginal states. Yet will it actually benefit them?

According to the free traders it will not, or at least only in the very short term. Tariffs were used successfully to build domestic industries, for example in Germany, France and the United States. Without them, it would have been difficult to compete with British manufactured goods. As Britain's industrialisation had come first, costs were lower and markets established, while Britannia ruled the waves with a navy which could outgun all others put together.

To use tariffs to prop up an ailing industry such as US steel, however, is less likely to deliver the goods. The problem is that protectionism does not here address the fundamental reasons for the industry's problems. On the contrary, it may remove the pressure to effect the kind of changes it needs to survive in the longer term.

Protectionism tends to favour those sectors of the economy with the most political muscle and these are unlikely to be the ones which must be developed if long-term interests are given priority. Steel corporations are long-established concentrations of wealth with enormous influence in both of America's main political parties. The United Steel Workers is a powerful union and the industry is one of the most unionised in a country where the labour movement overall is weak. So steel workers' jobs are preserved, but perhaps at the cost of others whose employers must now buy domestic steel more expensive than the pre-tariff imports.

Enthusiasts for free trade claim NAFTA generates economic activity and therefore brings jobs and prosperity. Opponents, on the other hand, argue that jobs will be lost in the US and Canada as companies relocate or out-source to Mexico. In addition, environmental law, social protection, health and safety and working conditions are all being dragged down by intensified cross-border competition. While free trade does bring prosperity to some, it also has clear losers. Some firms have undoubtedly expanded their markets as a result of being able to trade more freely with other countries. This has benefited their shareholders and, in some cases, their employees. At the same time, the downward pressure on standards as US, Canadian and Mexican enterprises compete more intensely is clearly evident.

The pro-globalisation view is that, in the medium-to-long term, trade liberalisation will increase overall prosperity and therefore produce far more winners than losers. The anti-globalisation view is that the process, deliberately furthered by powerful interests, is making it harder to achieve social justice and a higher degree of equality, undermining the power of democratic institutions and the ability of national governments to carry out the mandates upon which they were elected.

The Zapatista guerrilla army which emerged from the forests of Chiapas on the day that NAFTA came into force belongs to the latter group. The Zapatistas are simply more desperate than most, believing that the extension, as part of the new accord, of foreigners' right to buy land will undermine their traditional claims, taking away all they own, their dignity, their ability to feed themselves and giving them instead a precarious existence as rural day labourers or on the fringes of urban life.

Since the beginning of the Zapatista revolt, an international movement, whose participants range from prosperous middle-class western environmentalists to the very poorest farmers of the Indian subcontinent, has grown up that has in some ways sought to emulate it. For the Zapatistas are a new kind of movement not only in the substance of their demands, but in the fact that they are fighting not simply against their national government or armed forces but against an accord with the world's most powerful nation.

This is a revolt, in style as well as substance, for the age of globalisation. Its leader, who calls himself Subcommander Marcos, and always appears masked, is educated, in touch with all sorts of events and trends in the world. He is someone who feels and expresses a solidarity with oppressed people everywhere. He is cool, glamorous, an ideal icon for an age in which radical activists have made Che Guevara, the Subcommander Marcos of the 1950s and 1960s, into a secular saint. The mysterious choice of subcommander as his rank raised the question of who actually 'commanded' the Zapatistas. Was there a more powerful figure lurking in the background? Someone too old, perhaps, to do more than be the brains behind the movement? Was the idea that if Marcos were captured, he could be replaced by another 'subcommander,' because the real commander was elsewhere? Or was the commander the ghost of Zapata? Or some Aztec spirit returned like King Arthur to lead his (or her) people to freedom? Whatever the explanation, the mystery, or perhaps joke, seemed typical of what the anti-globalisation movement would become: playful, interested in form and ceremony, mingling hard-headed and determined radicalism with a sort of mysticism which had historically been anathema to most of the left.

Go to an anti-globalisation demonstration and you will see the red flags of the old left. You will see the green of an environmentalist movement which has grown hugely in the last two decades. You will see the black of the black blocs, of direct action and anarchism. But you will also see flags like rainbows, symbolising the unity of all, the red, green, yellow and black of Africa and Rastafarianism, the pink of gay pride, the crescent of Islam and the cross of Christianity.

The Zapatistas use the Internet with skill, and their Websites are linked to radical movements of every kind throughout the world. The fundamental value of their moral code is clear and it is also that of the anti-globalisation movement: solidarity. This solidarity extends beyond Marx's famous dictum, 'Workers of All Countries Unite!', though that was also uttered in response to a globalising age. It goes beyond black power, gay pride, women's liberation or animal rights, embracing all of these and more, a solidarity which rails against every species of oppression and exploitation, making links between previously disparate causes. How lasting this will prove, whether its very breadth will turn out to be a recipe for dissipation or the foundation of a durable strength, the next few years will surely tell us.

Saturday, 30 November 1999, Seattle: Huge street protests disrupt the World Trade Organisation's (WTO) ministerial meetings. The protests are different from anything seen before, at least on this scale, and in one crucial respect: diversity.

If the only people concerned about globalisation's implications were western blue collar workers, then the protests could have been written off as a sort of ghost dance, comparable to the futile spiritual 'uprising' which was the North American Indian's late-19th-century response to decades of military defeat and genocide. If people were willing to make cars for a tenth of the pay in South Korea or Brazil, then clearly cars would be made in those places and the US rust belt would get rustier. Resistance might be noble and romantic, but retraining would make more sense.

The same might have been the case if the only ones protesting at Seattle had been indigenous people from Central America or the Far East.

Of course, young people would be there with all sorts of bees in their bonnets. The young would always protest, or some of them would. In ten years time they'll be trying to hold down a job and raise a family, same as the rest of us.

And we all want to save the whale, that's why we have the International Whaling Commission.

This is how people who have never taken part in a demonstration tend to view them: labour defending its sectional interests; people left behind by history refusing to pass into oblivion without a fight; hard-headed folks trying to get an amendment attached to Article 44 of the Bill on something or other, so that that mine doesn't get to spill poison into their river – spill the stuff somewhere else, sure, but we don't want it; and young people and a few obsessives with the time and energy not only to care about turtles but to get out on to the street and show people they care.

Never before had these disparate malcontents appeared on the street together. Seattle was different. The variety of groups out on the streets of the United States' most north-westerly city was impressive: environmentalists, labour, solidarity groups, people who'd travelled not only from all over the country but from throughout the world to draw attention to their grievances, but not only to their grievances. Many were beginning to believe that they had a common enemy and that this enemy had names and faces. They saw that what threatened the tiger and the rain forest was what also threatened to reduce once-vibrant industrial cities to ghost towns: corporate business and its insatiable demand for markets, for profit, for a satisfactory bottom line. Teamsters and turtles united in common cause.

The euphoria of the day's coalition was always going to give way to something more measured, and there would be divisions in the alliance. When, two years later, US steel workers won their fight to have tariffs imposed on foreign imports, environmentalists were nowhere to be heard, though they might logically have been expected to celebrate a move which would reduce the international movement of a heavy commodity, and therefore cut, amongst other things, greenhouse gas emissions. When the 'War against Terror' led to the removal of long-standing freedoms, provoking protests from the sort of activist groups which had been most visible in Seattle, labour went along with it, not wanting to seem unpatriotic, or to question the President's trustworthiness at a time of war.

Yet the alliance had been very real, if limited, and the feeling of solidarity it had generated was something new. The coming together of interests in Seattle gave the WTO pause for thought. No one imagined that alone it would halt trade liberalisation in its tracks, but nor would it be without consequences.

Globalised resistance, is, paradoxically perhaps, itself a feature of globalisation, not only provoked by it but made possible by what it has to offer: cheap travel, satellite TV, the Internet, mobile phones. Alliances between different groups affected by this remaking of the world will often be transient, usually shifting and invariably difficult. Yet something was born at Seattle, and it revolved around a common suspicion: that whatever it is you want – to keep your job, to save the rain forest, to eat food you can trust, to be educated in your own language – you can only have it if somebody much more powerful than yourself, your family, your union or your community agrees. What the demonstrators in Seattle really had in common was this, a demand that democracy be given back its original meaning, that the peoples of the world reclaim the chance to participate in decisions which would affect their lives and the future of all of us.

Sunday, 26 December 1999, London: In a match against Southampton, Chelsea become the first English football club to field a team consisting entirely of foreign players. The Blues' team that Boxing Day contained men from The Netherlands, Norway, Italy, Spain, France, Brazil, Uruguay and Nigeria. Foreign players first arrived in the Britain in any numbers in the late 1980s, and by the mid-1990s they were commonplace. It was only a matter of time before someone put out eleven at once.

There are a number of reasons why English football clubs and foreign players like each other, most of which have to do with the fact that, since the advent of satellite television and the subsequent influx of huge sums of money into the game, the major English clubs – and some which aren't so major – have become very rich indeed and pay amongst the best wages. The changes which led to Chelsea's 'International XI' taking the field were, however, more profound than this would suggest.

Association Football, which has been played in most parts of the world for a century or more, has, through the media of television and global marketing, broken out of its national boundaries. The fans reflect the international awareness of clubs, players and media – though the fact that Middlesbrough supporters greeted their Brazilian star Juninho by wearing sombreros suggested that the details sometimes remain a little hazy. Fifty years ago almost all supporters followed their local side, and if you happened to come from Halifax rather than Wolverhampton, well, life wasn't always fair. Then, towards the end of the 1960s, televised football, which had been almost non-existent before the 1966 World Cup, began to become more common. All over the country children and teenagers rebelled. Why watch Halifax when you could watch Leeds, or Manchester United? Car ownership was growing and public transport was still comprehensive and reliable. People could afford to get around.

Lots of people still watch their local team, of course. Yet far more profess allegiance to big clubs which they rarely or never see play other than on TV, and sometimes ones whose names they can't even pronounce. When Manchester United visited their far less successful (but locally, at least as popular) neighbours Manchester City during the 2000-2001 season, City supporters held up a banner which read 'Welcome to Manchester,' while a Norwegian City player quipped that United were 'the pride of Singapore.'

The very biggest football clubs have become almost divorced from geography, existing in a borderless world where allegiances are determined by the most arbitrary of passing fancies, for a particular player, an eye-catching performance you happen to see on television, even a strip's colour scheme. Sustained success is, of course, a prerequisite. Falter and this kind of fan quickly looks elsewhere.

The globalisation of football is not simply a result of the existence of certain very wealthy clubs who can buy the best players. Whilst it may have economic and technological roots, it requires also sweeping changes in laws and practices. Until Britain joined the European Economic Community (EEC) in 1973 foreign players were a rarity in English football, simply because they were not allowed, under normal circumstances, to play here. Globalisation is something people do, not something which just happens to them, and this is as true for other, less glamorous sectors of the economy as it is for mass spectator sports.

With EEC membership came an immediate obligation to allow players who were citizens of other member states to sign for British clubs. Remaining restrictions were gradually eroded and by the end of the 1990s clubs within the European Union (EU) were entitled to sign players with EU passports under precisely the same conditions as would apply when dealing with their own nationals. When television companies began to pour money into the game in exchange for exclusive rights to show major tournaments, the clubs were able to take advantage of their new wealth by scouring Europe for the best players. English football was thus not 'globalised' by 'inexorable forces,' but by changes in the law brought about by powerful people seeking to take advantage of economic, technological and cultural developments.

2001, summer, any city in western Europe, North America, Australia, a score of other places: A young man and woman walk along a street towards a park. When they arrive they will join hundreds of others to listen to a Cora player from Mali, a group of Peruvians playing pan pipes, an Irish fiddle band, or perhaps a Trinidadian fusion of Jamaican ska and Brazilian samba. They have never lived anywhere but in this city, but fifty years ago, before their parents arrived, people would have turned to look at them, astonished to see two people who were clearly from so far away.

Neither of them has much money, but they appear well-dressed, in clothes with well-known labels, trademarks from America, Germany or Italy. In reality the clothes were made in the Far East, or Eastern Europe, under licence from transnational corporations (TNCs) with their head offices in the US or EU. When the couple arrive at the park they will eat snacks recognisably related to traditional foods from India, China, Vietnam, Mexico, Turkey or Morocco. These same foods will be assembled from ingredients originating in a wide variety of sources: meat from South America, spices from Indonesia, flour from North America, sugar from the Caribbean. Perhaps the girl will call her friends to get them to come and meet them. She'll call on a telephone bearing a Finnish brand name, but it will have been assembled somewhere a very long way from Finland. In a single day our couple could well have used or experienced something – food, clothing, music, technology – from almost every country in the world. Every purchase made, moreover, will have a tiny effect on the global economy, linking together the world's billions in a matrix of extraordinary complexity.

The matrix has many sides, many junctions, billions of inputs and uncountable possible outcomes. It is a matrix of rich cultural interchange, a merging of styles and ways that has given us new forms of art, literature and music, that allows anyone with a satellite dish to watch the best (and worst) of everything from everywhere, that has made international travel no longer the province of the rich. But it is also a matrix of exploitation and poverty, greed and indifference.

Summer, 2002, everywhere you look: Caceres in the Extremadura region of Spain in May, Athens in June, Reading in July, Singapore in August, Sicily and South Africa in September – the World Organisation for Music and Dance, WOMAD for short, holds its festivals of 'World music.' And WOMAD is only one of a number of groups promoting music from every country you can name.

From Woodstock to the 1980s, if you went to a rock festival anywhere in the world the chances were that almost all the bands playing would come from North America, Britain or other English-speaking countries, whilst the rest would be trying to sound as if they did. Gradually exceptions appeared: Jamaican ska, Andean pan pipes, Portuguese fado. Then fusions grew up, sometimes because of migration: West Indian music influenced by British rock, and vice versa, Latino traditions responding to the host cultures of the USA, American blues men travelling through Africa to search for the roots of their music and returning home with new sounds, new instruments, new ideas. In the end what emerged was not only a fusion of styles between, say, West Africa and New Orleans, but an eclectic whirlpool of musical traditions and inventiveness which was wholly new and in which might be heard echoes of a myriad ways of making people dance, think, feel, smile and weep.

Surely, here at last is an example of globalisation which has no parallel in the past, which cannot be castigated as simply the modern manifestation of what in the 19th century produced the great western-dominated empires, or in the 20th century allowed certain powerful industrial nations to call the shots, even as colonialism in the literal sense faded and died. World music is about mutual respect, about producing something exciting and fresh from inside a globalised aesthetic which was open to all and in which all could meet as equals. Or is it?

The answer turns out to be complicated, contentious and ever shifting – much like every other aspect of globalisation discussed in this book.

Musicians have shared experiences, ideas and techniques since prehistoric times. Though modern communications have brought new sounds to the ears of the world, this is less something wholly new than it is an intensification of something visible – or audible – throughout human history. Musicians have always had the advantage of being unbound by language. Rock music itself brings together traditions which can be traced back to Africa, to Ireland, to Spain and a hundred other countries and regions. Country music took Celtic sounds and subjected them to the influence of the emerging black folk forms of jazz and blues, as well as to Cajun, the Irish, English and Scottish ballad tradition, and anything else that happened to pass the ears of white popular entertainers in the southern states of the US. West African slaves, forbidden to use drums by nervous slave owners, adapted East African hand-clapping techniques and planted the seed of gospel. Latin America and Africa began to interact musically shortly after the first Europeans crossed the Atlantic and have kept it up ever since. Much further back, instruments and influences followed the Silk Road, bringing together sounds from China, Persia, Turkey and Italy. And in 19th- and early 20th-century Europe, 'classical' composers looked to folk traditions to provide a soundtrack for an emerging progressive nationalism, or simply for inspiration. The great religions spread certain ways of doing music – and taboos on certain other ways – around the globe. Music was certainly a feature of that earlier globalisation based on opening the world to trade, based on trafficking in human beings, on territorial expansion and war, and it undoubtedly had its role in still earlier 'globalisations,' of Greek and Roman cultures, of Christianity and Islam, of history's great Diaspora, migrations voluntary, forced and somewhere between the two.

Closer scrutiny of the actual relationships involved must lead at least to a certain questioning of the optimistic view of the process outlined above. Why, for example, is it called 'world music'? The label recalls Louis Armstrong's famous remark that all music was 'folk music' because "I ain't never heard a hoss sing." Why is music from Lesotho 'world music' but that from Liverpool not? The term reflects the same kind of Eurocentric view which has confined the description 'ethnic' to certain parts of humanity and, indeed, to their music and other arts. A Peruvian playing the pan pipes is a legitimate study for 'ethnomusicology'; a Yorkshireman playing a trumpet isn't. The result of this mentality is that, while many examples of genuine collaboration between western musicians and those from other parts of the world can be found, so can the exploitative, the derivative and the downright false. In world music, as in every aspect of western culture, exoticism can lead to human beings becoming transformed into mere symbols: the 'noble savage,' the 'authentic,' a repository for all the failed and vain hopes of western society's malcontents, or the moneymaking schemes of the powerful. As much as the Zapatista rebellion, 'world music' can perhaps be said to exemplify globalisation, warts and all.

1: Definitions

'…things that people hostile to the modern economy don't like.'

John Kay [1]

For Alan Greenspan of the US Federal Reserve, it's a 'prosperity-enhancing sea-change in world markets.' [2] For Rabbi Jonathan Sacks, it's 'the latest buzzword of the west.' [3] For radical writers James Petras and Henry Veltmeyer, it is a process through which 'the existing world economic order is… being renovated so as to create optimal conditions for the free play of greed, class interest and profit-making.' As a set of ideas, it is no more than an 'attempt to throw an ideological veil over the economic interests of an emerging class of transnational capitalists.' [4] For some, it is a process to be celebrated, a coming together of the human race for peaceful ends, a growing interdependence based on trade, mutual respect, a sharing and merging of cultures. For others, it is an old devil in new clothes, a system controlled by the powerful in their own interests, the exploitation of weak nations by strong, the obliteration of traditional cultures in favour of the glitz and pap of Hollywood.

Most mainstream analysts have defined globalisation as a complex phenomenon made up of a number of parallel processes, each of which grows, more or less inevitably, out of changes which are themselves beyond control. In this view, globalisation may be either welcomed or lamented, but it must, in the end, be accepted. Changes in telecommunications, transport, in how things are made and the way people think have led inexorably to a world in which information and capital can travel from continent to continent instantly, people in hours and goods in a matter, at most, of days.

This, these theorists argue, has economic effects: it means economies must become more competitive, by increasing productivity or driving down costs. It has political effects: it makes the traditional welfare state no longer viable and increases the power of corporations to dictate to governments by threatening to relocate or disinvest if they don't get their way. And it has had cultural effects: it brings the sounds of western pop music to the remotest places and 'world music' to the west, allows CNN to broadcast an American view of the world to anyone with a television and a satellite dish, enables the relentless spread of brand names: McDonald's, Nike, Microsoft, Coca-Cola, Marlboro, Manchester United, *The Simpsons*. We might not like any of this, but all we can do is try to alleviate its worst effects and make the best of the good it might bring.

Outside of this consensus, however, can be heard a chorus of voices of people who, from a range of points of view, reject the idea that globalisation is either beneficial or inevitable. Some claim that the whole thing is 'globaloney,' simply an attempt to convince people that, in the words of a globally famous American TV series, 'Resistance is futile.' Petras and Veltmeyer argue that the concept of 'inevitability' is central to the ideological function of globalisation, a notion 'presented with an air of inevitability that disarms the imagination and prevents thoughts of action towards a systemic alternative – towards another, more just social and economic order.' [5] Others argue that, while there is certainly something going on that might be called 'globalisation,' it is anything but inevitable. As economics writer John Kay sees it, 'Few components of globalisation are inevitable if there is a popular will to stop them. Mostly there is not.' [6] This, however, ignores powerful forces standing in the way of the development of a popular will sufficiently clear, strong and united to halt what is now called globalisation, or to take control of the process and transform it: firstly, it is not always obvious to people, especially those with no access to higher levels of education, that the loss of their farm, their job, their local common land or their hospital is connected to the ambitions of rich investors on the other side of the world. Secondly, people may well understand what is going on and who is to blame but, preferring to stay alive and with all limbs and faculties intact, choose to stay quietly bent over their sewing machines, ploughs or VDUs, thinking their own thoughts.

Broadly, as well as a mingling of cultures, globalisation is seen as involving economic deregulation, trade liberalisation and corporate domination. In addition, globalisation has its own institutions: the United Nations clearly plays a role in this, as does the NATO military alliance, but the stars of the show are the International Monetary Fund (IMF), the World Bank, and, arguably the most important of all, the World Trade Organisation (WTO). Globalisation has also seen a weakening of the power of working people and their movements, and a strengthening of the position of employers. Not everyone sees this as a bad thing, but few question that it is happening.

Since the end of the 1970s the world has seen widespread economic deregulation, the liberalisation of markets and trade, and a greater political-economic uniformity. Not only has the Communist bloc been vastly diminished, but what remains of it (currently with the sole exception of North Korea) has been forced, to one degree or another, to come to terms with capitalism. Where there were once two superpowers, one of them based upon an aggressive, vibrant market economy and the other on a rigorous, authoritarian, top-down collectivism, there is now only one. At the same time, western social democratic and labour parties have been forced to water down or even abandon their traditional approach, which tended to involve pursuing reforms to make the market economy fairer whilst in practice accepting that capitalism was here to stay, and even that it was a necessary condition of a free and open society.

Alongside these developments, the balance of power between states and private corporations has shifted in favour of the latter. Again, some regard this as inevitable whilst others argue that Transnational Corporations (TNCs) appear more powerful than governments only because they have in effect taken them over, that both are run by people with identical interests who went to the same schools and often even come from the same families. Whatever the truth of this, it is worth noting that General Motors' annual sales are worth more than the total GDP of a large middle-income country such as Turkey or South Africa, or a small, rich nation like Denmark. The top five corporations have sales over three times as great as the combined GDP of the whole of sub-Saharan Africa. [7] This does not, despite many assertions to the contrary, mean that they are more powerful. It is, for one thing, not a comparison of like with like – sales represent the total value of goods exchanged for cash, whilst GDP only measures value added. Nevertheless, it gives some idea of the scale of the modern corporation.

The weakening of state power to the advantage of TNCs has brought about a corresponding increase in the power of multinational institutions, primarily the World Bank, IMF and WTO. These bodies, aided and abetted by more specialised international organisations and by regional institutions working to the same agenda, have grown to become a kind of nascent world government, and one which is almost wholly beyond democratic control.

Corporations have gained power not only at the expense of states, but also in relation to the people they employ. During the 1980s, the application of new technologies transformed the way in which many goods were produced, raised labour productivity and enabled corporations to shed large numbers of employees, weakening trade unions. In Britain and the US Prime Minister Thatcher and President Reagan forced home this advantage with a series of actions designed to break the back of the labour movement. In Britain, neither organised labour nor the social democratic politics it favoured ever recovered from the huge defeat of the 1984-85 miners' strike. In the United States, Ronald Reagan took on airline pilots and won, demonstrating to workers with far less bargaining power than these highly skilled specialists that they had better not mess with him.

The decline of workers' power is reflected by the fact that real wages in the United States have not risen since 1971. Internationally, it can be seen in the falling share of national income taken by wage earners in most countries, especially developing countries which have seen IMF-dictated Structural Adjustment Programmes (SAPs). SAPs generally involve thoroughgoing economic deregulation, an end to most government subsidies and, through privatisation, the retreat of the state from whole areas of the economy. Employment protection laws have to be weakened because hard to fire means reluctant to hire. And if the government is basically on the employers' side, workers who can be sacked more or less at will are less likely to demand pay rises or to get them if they do.

The IMF welcomes the relative inability of employees to force up their own wages, since the Fund's favoured theory indicates that, for an economy to take off, capital must take a higher share of national income. This capital then becomes available for reinvestment, and this benign recycling leads to economic take-off, to everyone's eventual advantage.

Unfortunately, in the absence of exchange controls, which have all but disappeared from the globalising economy, there is no guarantee that capital will remain in the country in which it is generated. In fact, most of the profit made in developing countries finds its way back to the metropolitan North and into the bank accounts of TNC shareholders. The servicing and repayment of debt (which costs sub-Saharan African countries, for example, a fifth of their GDP each year) and the privatisation of resources (which results in foreign ownership and a fall in the share of wealth paid in wages) mean that far more capital flows out of poor countries than arrives in the form of direct investment or development aid.

There is, moreover, a quite different route to increased investment, and it was the one generally chosen by developed countries in the process of reconstruction which followed the Second World War. Simply pay people decent wages and make it worth their while to save, and they will save. At the same time make sure that your tax take is sufficient to cover the costs of providing, through public investment, everything that an efficient modern economy needs: transport infrastructure, healthcare, education, pensions and so on. This is the kind of programme most readily associated with social democracy, which in British terms means the Labour Party, but it was in fact based on a consensus of centre-left and centre-right which was as impossible to question in its day as the monetarist orthodoxy of the IMF is supposed to be in ours.

Such a course is no longer available to any country which seeks to play a full role in international commerce because the IMF, the WTO and the powerful governments and corporate players which stand behind them simply forbid it. There is an idea that welfare states are no longer 'affordable' but there is little if any evidence to support this. The Organisation for Economic Cooperation and Development (OECD) regularly publishes economic indicators which demonstrate that there is no correlation one way or another between the proportion of GDP spent on social welfare and the overall performance of an economy. Typically cited as the most competitive economies of the last decade are the United States, Australia, Denmark, Ireland, The Netherlands and Norway. This is a mixed bag indeed, with the US having relatively paltry social provision, Norway, The Netherlands and Denmark amongst the world's most generous, and Australia and Ireland somewhere between. [8] The only conclusion is that competitiveness and growth are neither necessarily derived from, nor hindered by, the existence of an effective and well-funded welfare state.

Coupled with the available new technologies, and fuelled by a continuing supply of affordable oil made possible by the United States' successful geopolitics, the narrowing of options for developing countries and the imposition of a single development model have made possible a new global system of production. This system has several elements: a marked reduction in the price of transport and communication; partly as a result of this, a new international division of labour, in which more and more production is moved to low-wage countries; and the development of manufacturing in developing countries whose role in the world economy was until recently confined to the production of food and raw materials.

Considered in this light the idea that globalisation is a 'natural' or 'inevitable' process seems to have little going for it. Certainly, technological developments have made a particular form of globalisation available; taking advantage of that availability has, however, involved decisions taken by real living, breathing human beings who could have taken other decisions had they felt these were in their interests or for some other reason desirable. 'Inevitability' and democracy simply cannot coexist. There would be no point in seeking a popular mandate to repeal the Second Law of Thermodynamics. If globalisation is inevitable, then the best a government could hope to achieve would be to pursue policies which give its people, and the industries which employ them, the edge in adjusting to it. You cannot vote against an earthquake, but you can ensure that buildings take account of the danger and that every effort is made to minimise loss of life. It does not seem, however, that globalisation and the shocks it brings are comparable.

Calling globalisation's bluff on the question of inevitability should lead us to question other aspects of the phenomenon. Trade is growing, of that there can be no doubt, and at a far greater rate than the overall economic output. Yet is this truly the 'engine of prosperity' which the globalisers claim it to be, and can liberalisation claim the credit for it? The value of world trade in goods grew from under $3.5 trillion in 1990 to reach about $5.5 trillion in 1997. [9] Though it grew less sharply as the world flirted with recession in 2001, the secular trend may well continue. World output grew in real terms at an average annual rate of only 3.7% between 1948 and 1997 compared with world trade growth of 6%. Between 1950 and 1997, international trade flows multiplied by a factor of 17, while output increased sixfold. [10]

As these figures demonstrate, trade has been growing since the end of the Second World War, both in absolute terms and as a proportion of overall economic activity. Yet before the early 1970s, protectionist policies were the norm, and a huge proportion of the world's population lived in the Soviet bloc, China, or other countries whose approach to commerce, based as it was on relations between planned economies, was very different to the conditions of trade between capitalist nations. In addition, many developing countries saw import substitution, whereby domestically-produced goods replace imports, as the key to greater prosperity. Economic ideologies – socialist economic planning, liberalisation of trade, Keynesian interventionism in various guises, protectionism of different kinds, and all manner of combinations of these broad schools of thought – competed with each other on the political, economic, social and on occasions military stage. The average tariff on imported manufactured goods was 47% in 1947. This had fallen to 6% by 1980 and now stands at a little over 3%. [11] Yet economic growth overall shows no tendency to correlate with this reduction in the most significant and visible barrier to trade. The apparent triumph of a single orthodoxy does not appear to have accelerated the growth of global prosperity.

Although this is true on the global level, it does not apply to all countries, some of which have indeed seen external trade grow in importance. Significantly, one of these is the United States. This is a major change historically, because what first made the US rich was its huge domestic market and resources. Since the 1980s, however, Americans have traded with increasing enthusiasm with the rest of the world. The United States still does proportionally less trade than do other developed countries, yet despite this it is the world's largest exporter of merchandise and services. In 2000, total US trade reached $2.5 trillion, up from $2.17 trillion just three years earlier. Total exports were $1.4 trillion, while imports were a record $1.1 trillion. [12] This sounds impressive, until you consider that America's total GDP was touching $9 trillion by the turn of the century. In addition, the bulk of this trade is not global but hemispheric, and with the accession of the Free Trade Area of the Americas, a wider agreement designed to succeed NAFTA, it is likely to become more so. In this respect, moreover, the USA is not untypical: globalisation or no, almost all countries' major trading parties are neighbouring states.

The US economy, even more than most, is dominated by TNCs. Unlike the situation in most countries, however, TNCs active in the United States are also the country's own leading domestic firms. In 2000, despite difficulties in the broader economy, America's TNCs dominated the global economy, with 185 in *Fortune* magazine's famous Top 500, compared to 179 in 1999. [13] Yet if these mega-corporations provide the motor of the globalising economy, they paradoxically continue to earn most of their profits at home. This, however, is beginning to change, with overseas earnings growing to become a balance-book item difficult to replace through domestic development, however competitive one's products. This in part explains why the United States has become so keen to promote global free trade, though it tends to employ a somewhat one-sided interpretation of this term, allowing the US to continue to exclude certain categories of Third World product, and impose significant tariffs when it suits it to do so.

The growth in significance of international trade is thus a phenomenon which, if certainly real enough, must be qualified: it applies only to some countries and some commodities; it may be exaggerated by another aspect of globalisation, the fact that we are all increasingly subjected to US views of the world, and for Americans the growth of trade has been real and important; and most trade continues to be conducted on the regional level rather than on a scale we might consider 'global.'

There is, however, one aspect of the international economy where globalisation is certainly evident as a transforming force: finance. Linking investor and productive facility is now an array of banks, finance institutions of various degrees of legitimacy, tax havens, currency and commodity traders, and speculators great and small. It is perhaps this which, at least after its highly visible impact on our cultures, most people would think of when they hear the word 'globalisation': financial transactions spanning the globe in nanoseconds, huge sums of money moving from market to market at the speed of light, high-technology communications systems making it all possible. Between 1981 and 1995 Foreign Direct Investment (FDI) increased sixfold globally. Total borrowing on international capital markets increased by a factor of around eight during the same period. Between the mid-1970s and the mid-1990s the daily turnover on foreign exchange markets went up from a mere billion dollars to 1,200 times that figure. [14] And dominating the world financial scene are the two great markets of London and New York, which together account for almost half of the world's transactions. Presiding over all of this activity, moreover, are public and private international financial institutions, institutions whose reach is truly global.

This liberalisation of capital movements has contributed to another marked feature of globalisation, the spread of the internationally-recognised brand name. A combination of shrewd investment, ruthlessly anti-competitive policies, aggressive marketing and, in some cases, cultural adaptability has, for example, made a number of retail outlets ubiquitous across the globe. Franchising sucks in local entrepreneurial talent, draining capital from both developing and developed countries, incorporating potential rivals and tying the interests of local elites to those of big corporations, most of which are based in the US. Whereas manufacturers of big ticket items from aeroplanes to cars to weaponry have reorganised the global economy by dispersing and outsourcing production of different components, this is impossible for most of the service sector. Yet businesses for whom production and consumption are inherently localised – retail and fast food outlets, service providers such as car hire and public transport firms, office cleaners, and accountants, to take a few examples – are being reorganised through privatisation, consolidation, takeover and merger to provide internationally recognisable brand names and products. This activity is led by the financial services industries, and without rapid and reliable ways of moving capital around it would not be possible

Notes

1. *Financial Times*, 14 November 2001
2. 'Global Economic Integration: Opportunities And Challenges,' Remarks by Chairman Alan Greenspan at a symposium sponsored by the Federal Reserve Bank of Kansas City, Jackson Hole, Wyoming, 25 August 2000, at <http://www.federalreserve.gov/boarddocs/speeches/2000/20000825.htm>
3. *The Guardian*, 19 December 2001
4. *Globalization Unmasked: Imperialism In The 21st Century* (Zed Books, 2001) p.8
5. *Globalization Unmasked: Imperialism In The 21st Century* (Zed Books, 2001) p.8
6. *Financial Times*, 14 November 2001
7. *New Internationalist*, issue 296, 1999, at <http://www.newint.org/issue296/facts.html>
8. See, for example; *The New Economy: First Report On The OECD Growth Project*, 14 June 2000 at <http://www1.oecd.org/subject/growth/new_eco.pdf>
9. *United Nations World Economic and Social Survey 1998*
10. *WTO Annual Report 1998*
11. *New Internationalist*, issue 296, 1999, at <http://newint.org/issue296/facts.html>
12. California Chamber of Commerce International Trade Statistics at <http://www.calchamber.com/business_resources/international_statistics.htm>
13. Fortune Global 500: The World's Largest Corporations, at <http://www.fortune.com/indexw.jhtml>
14. *New Internationalist*, issue 296, 1999, at <http://newint.org/issue296/facts.html>

2: Globalisation Then And Now

'Constant revolutionising of production, uninterrupted distur-
bance of social conditions, everlasting uncertainty and agita-
tion... All that is solid melts into air... All old-established
national industries have been destroyed or are daily being
destroyed. They are dislodged by new industries, whose introduction becomes a life and death question for all civilised
nations, by industries that no longer work up indigenous raw
material, but raw material drawn from the remotest zones;
industries whose products are consumed not only at home, but
in every quarter of the globe. In place of the old wants, satisfied
by the productions of the country, we find new wants, requiring
for their satisfaction the products of distant lands and climes. In
place of the old local and national seclusion we have intercourse
in every direction, universal interdependence of nations.'

Karl Marx and Friedrich Engels,
The Manifesto Of The Communist Party, 1848

From about the 15th century up until the rapid industrialisation of Britain
in the late 1700s, a kind of 'globalisation' occurred which, though it differed in many respects from its modern equivalent, had also much in common with it. Wealth from colonial cotton, from the slave trade, from trade in
high value commodities such as spices, coffee and precious metals, helped
to provide the capital needed to ignite the fires of the industrial revolution.
In relative terms, however, industrialisation in Britain and other western
nations reduced this flow of capital as more and more wealth was both produced (in mills, mines, factories, shipyards and so on) and consumed
(through an ever-increasing standard of living) at home.

During the phase of rapid international economic growth which lasted
from around the beginning of the 1890s until the outbreak of the First World
War, trade in goods was at greater proportional levels than it is today and
made a much more significant contribution to growth than it now does. It
was in this period that industrial conglomerates enjoying near-monopolies
of production emerged, consolidated finance houses wielding immense
amounts of capital were established, and corporations began their rise to
international dominance. It also saw the peak of colonialism and the pene-
tration of a huge proportion of the planet's surface by a particular set of economic relationships, a particular way of doing and making things. Again,

some aspects of this have changed, but the pattern remains: if colonialism itself has been largely dismantled, the unequal economic relationships involved persist.

While industrial capitalism was out conquering the world, it was also transforming the way things were done and made back home. From the 1890s onwards workers were increasingly likely to be employed in large industrial units using mass production methods such as conveyer belt assembly, multiple shifts and mechanisation. To these were added 'Taylorism,' a 'scientific' approach to management which sought to minimise the amount of labour needed to produce goods, for example through time-and-motion study and rational task design.

It is hardly controversial to say that the well-being of their employees was not the paramount consideration of such techniques or of the men who applied them. To defend their interests in the face of this, workers created trade unions which collectivised their bargaining power and evened up the odds between labour and capital. When their right to organise was persistently threatened, they began to seek political representation, so that anti-union laws would be harder to enact and maintain. When they saw that what could be achieved through purely workplace-based organisation was limited, they created political parties to further their broader interests.

Such parties might be long on revolutionary rhetoric, but in practice they were generally short of such fervour when it came to action. Instead, they attempted to win a greater share of resources for working people through existing legal and political structures and without challenging the right of owners of capital to continue to run their businesses and industries. In country after country, parties won seats in parliaments and local authorities on the basis of a political programme of redistribution of wealth and the creation of welfare states. Eventually, many won power.

The inter-war period saw changes to the pattern of consumption as well as on the productive side of the equation. Before the late 19th century, mass markets in the modern sense did not exist. The vast bulk of the population throughout the world, including in the industrialising West, simply had no surplus income: men and women provided for their own and their families' most basic needs – food, clothing, shelter – and once having done so had nothing left to spend.

In the last quarter of the 19th century a growing proportion of working people in western Europe, Britain and America experienced the first stirrings of prosperity. They remained poor, of course, but many were no longer so mired in poverty that every farthing had to be dedicated to survival. In addition, the extraordinary hours many had to work in order to secure a living wage were giving way to days which remained long, but nevertheless allowed time for some kind of a life. One result of this was a vibrant mass culture which brought music halls, street parades, spectator sport. Child labour was reduced and basic education became virtually ubiquitous, bringing with it an awareness of the wider world. Whilst manufacturers and retailers attempted to separate the citizen from his or her pay, philanthropists (often the same people) promoted sobriety and learning through public libraries, popular lectures on science and the arts, and religious observance.

Advertising, which had probably existed as long as the exchange of goods, tended to emphasise quality and durability. Frippery remained largely a province of the rich. This did not change substantially until after the First World War when, using techniques based on the new 'science' of psychoanalysis, American 'public relations' men – a wholly new profession – began to understand that, if people had more money to spend on non-essentials, then what they spent it on could be determined, with a little shove in the right direction, by irrational, manipulable impulses rather than through the hard-headed investment and labour-saving principles which had fuelled demand for hard-wearing boots, for sewing machines and more wholesome food. Not only had incomes risen, but cheap materials and mass production techniques had made it possible for working people to aspire to own glamorous-looking clothes, radios and gramophone players, and to eat for pleasure as well as need.

Thus was consumerism born, the guiding principle of a society whose leaders had learnt not so much, as is so often claimed, to control the crowd in the manner of a Hitler or Mosley, but in fact by dividing people, atomising them so that they perceived first and foremost their needs and desires as individuals. Collectivism had till then characterised labour's early response to its plight, looking to socialism to bring a better world for all or, failing that, at least more frequent trams or a shorter working day. Trapped in a system which made individual social mobility all but impossible, working people had little choice but to look for organised, united means of improving their lot.

Until after the First World War, collectivist political philosophies had few rivals for the allegiance of the mass of people: to escape the prison of mine, mill or factory, you could, through unionism, throw your lot in with others in the same situation, you could look to the Lord to help, or you could look for solace in a bottle or pint glass. Consumerism added another option, and in the long run it rode parasitically to dominance on the back of the success of its collectivist rival. Collectivist political philosophies enabled working people to gain a far greater share of the world's growing wealth than would otherwise have been possible. Yet when people found this new wealth in their pockets, they chose to spend it on the fulfilment of their dreams not through Red Revolution, but through the accumulation of possessions, through consumption.

Events during and after the World War of 1914-18 had made it quite urgent for the ideologues of the market economy to find a way to counter the possible spread of left-wing ideas. Although most working people in the world showed little interest in the revolutionary overthrow of capitalism, the fact that this had happened in Russia in 1917, and that an economy and society organised on very different lines to those of the free market west existed and, for a time, appeared to be flourishing, had a major impact. The Soviet Union in the 1930s was a hard place to present as the ideal society of the future, but exactly how it might look to people in the west depended very much on who they were and what their priorities may have been. To most (though not all) educated, well-to-do people, to intellectuals and others who valued their freedom of expression highly, and to the rich who wanted to hang on to what they had, it looked like a hell-hole of gulags, show trials and forced migration. But the USSR also had full employment, and to the man or woman waiting in a bread line in New York or Manchester, Paris or Berlin, such considerations may have seemed like a luxury.

As well as Soviet-style communism, another challenge to what would become the globally dominant economic system came in the wake of decolonisation. As empires were dismantled following the Second World War, most former colonies reacted to their years under foreign domination by extending state control of the economy and attempting to keep foreign corporations either out, or at least under close supervision. An economic model based on nationalisation, attempts to industrialise (in some cases almost from scratch) and modernise behind walls of protective tariffs and quotas became ubiquitous in the Third World. The theory was that in this way a domestic market could be developed, offering the population an inclusive well-being, security and the hope of a better life. Further, these achievements would be sustainable, because eventually domestic industries, having grown strong in their incubators of protection, would be able to go out into the world and compete.

One result of this variety of social and economic systems was that working people in different countries stood in various relationships to the systems of production of which they were the driving force. In our own times, the vast majority of people who are not, by the standards of their own societies, rich – this would embrace everyone from the poorest day labourer to the prosperous white collar middle class of a modern western city – are wage workers. Yet this has not always been the case. By International Labour Organisation estimates, the number of direct wage earners in the world rose from under two billion in 1980 to almost three billion by the mid-1990s. [1] Unfortunately, much of this labour has moved from self-employment and tenancy on small farms, and it has not done so voluntarily. Forced off the land through a combination of often subsidised food exports from rich countries, and food 'aid' either poorly planned or carried out with no thought to the welfare of indigenous farmers, people have no choice but to move to already overburdened cities in search of work or to migrate to the North, with all the risks, dangers and humiliations that almost invariably entails. Demand for labour has failed to keep pace with this supply, with the result that unemployment on a global level is estimated to have reached 1.5 billion. [2]

At the same time, the welfare systems and labour laws which can give wage earners a reasonably secure livelihood have come under severe pressure. Though the European Union proclaims its attachment to the 'European model,' in which a free market system is tempered by redistributive social policies, it is nevertheless the case that the comprehensive, cradle-to-grave welfare systems which arose after World War Two are being eroded and the logic of the market is becoming more pervasive.

Until the 1980s elections in liberal democracies offered the voters a choice of clearly differing economic philosophies and strategies. By the end of the century, however, the dominant assumption on centre-left as much as centre-right was that free market capitalism is not only the only route to prosperity, and therefore desirable on economic grounds, but that it will function best if unhampered by the kind of social obligations without which welfare states cannot exist. Far from there being any inherent conflict of interests between the profit motive which drives business and the general good, the former is seen as essential to the latter. What's good for business is good for everyone, and this is as true in Mongolia as it is in Manhattan, as essential to the continued prosperity of the richest countries as it is to the development of the poorest. This is the core belief of globalisation as not merely a process which we can observe and discuss, but a set of beliefs, an ideology as distinct and coherent as the great social and political systems which arose in the 19th and 20th centuries, one of which, Liberalism, is its direct ancestor.

Liberalism, moreover, and the modified version now known as neoliberalism, do not favour free market capitalism only because it is a route to prosperity. On the contrary, liberalism's core belief is that to trade, to enter into commercial activity aimed at the accumulation of wealth, to invest where and in what one wishes, are basic human rights. The fact that they lead to prosperity is extremely welcome, but the fact that they are essential aspects of freedom, as essential as free speech or freedom of worship, is, ultimately, of more fundamental importance.

Neoliberalism, and the belief that there is only one good way to run an economy, can be seen in retrospect to have begun their march to ascendancy in response to the crises that wracked the world at the end of the 1960s. For almost a quarter of a century after the end of the war, the western world enjoyed an unprecedented era of rising prosperity and social peace. The social peace came to a shuddering end with a series of spectacular, violent events; and while prosperity continued to increase, the price which was having to be paid for it – in increasing socio-economic division and environmental degradation – began to seem greater and greater.

In the United States five devastating political assassinations – of President John F. Kennedy and his brother Robert Kennedy, and the three black civil rights leaders Medgar Evers, Malcolm X and Martin Luther King – occurred within a period of just six years. King's, in particular, sparked off riots which seemed likely to lead to full scale insurrection. The assassinations and resultant riots were only the most spectacular manifestations of a burgeoning social unrest which united alienated urban blacks with draft resisters from white, middle-class families. While the Vietnam War distorted the US economy and disaffected swathes of the country's youth, it occurred also at a time of intensifying economic competition as a revitalised Japan burst onto the world scene, hotly pursued by a reconstructed Europe with, in a supreme irony, West Germany as its leading industrial power.

On 15 August 1971, responding to the ongoing drain of resources that was the Vietnam War, President Richard Nixon killed the Bretton Woods-organised world system of finance and trade with a single stroke of his pen. No longer would the dollar back up the convertibility of the world's currencies. Before Bretton Woods, currencies were given value and stability by their relationship to the gold held in each country's national treasury. After Bretton Woods the relationship became less direct, with the US dollar acting as a reserve currency for the world. After 15 August 1971, currencies became in a sense wholly fictional money. Each note has value only because a government (or, in the case of the recently-established Euro, group of governments and the European Central bank) guarantees that it has such value. Confidence in currencies thus relies, more than at any time in the history of the world, on politics, in a belief that value can be guaranteed by human-created institutions.

The result has been an unprecedented level of currency volatility and a new impetus to international co-operation. Only together can national banks and governments ensure the kind of stability necessary for continued economic growth and activity. Put that way, this sounds like a wholly positive development. Yet like so much else its actual effects are contingent upon power. In other words, 'co-operation' becomes too often a euphemism for a world in which the powerful call the shots. A brief examination of the direction in which income flows – profit, rent, royalties for patent use and so on – undermines the argument that, whereas imperialism was about dependence, globalisation is about interdependence. In fact, it hasn't changed, continuing to go from South to North, East to West, poor to rich.

The end of Bretton Woods did not signify the end of the institutions it had created but merely a development of their role. From the 1970s onwards, pressure mounted for the construction of a system of free movement of currency. Exchange controls would have to go. With the removal of exchange controls, governments became increasingly vulnerable to concerted attempts by speculators to influence their policies. The strike had always been labour's weapon: people who had little power within social hierarchies understood that the fact that they made everything gave them some kind of bargaining strength. The 1970s saw the advent of a new kind of strike, the investment strike. Countries following policies which were regarded as insufficiently business-friendly were likely to find capital flowing outwards at a dangerous rate. Disinvestment might also mean relocation: the threat to close plant and move production to places where labour was cheaper and politicians more compliant.

In three decades this has developed into a new international division of labour, in which low-wage countries are no longer relied upon, as in the traditional system, more or less exclusively for a supply of primary commodities, the products of farms, fisheries, mines and quarries. Instead, aided by plummeting transport costs and improved communications, they have become also sources of fully manufactured goods. In the mid-1990s a worker in Vietnam cost less than a sixtieth the price of a worker in the developed world.

The result was that one of two things happened: either, as in the case of cars, new production facilities were developed which had the advantage always enjoyed by newcomers. Not being burdened by previous investment in now outdated plant, they entered the market with state-of-the-art production technology and, of course, relatively cheap labour. Firms based in South Korea and later other far eastern countries, as well as of course in Japan, thus found that they could make better and cheaper cars than longer-established US rivals. The American response was a mix of aggressive investment tactics enabling US capital to cut itself a slice of the new pie, so that apparently far eastern-based TNCs were partly, and sometimes mainly, American-owned. Or, the strategy which was popular with clothing manufacturers, production moved abroad whilst retaining other parts of their activities in America. As *Financial Times* pundit John Kay has noted, '...US firms such as Gap and Compaq realised that an American brand and offshore manufacture made an unbeatable combination.' Thus, 'Jobs migrated from the US to the developing world.' [3]

The globalisation of production accompanied the rise of speculation. When exchange controls virtually disappeared countries rich and poor competed to attract inward investment, and increasingly tailored their policies to serve this goal. As a result the daily turnover on the foreign exchange (forex) markets rose from a mere billion dollars in the mid-1970s to $1.2 trillion by the mid-1990s. [4] These developments were facilitated by the emergence of a growing number of offshore centres, countries whose laws were tailored precisely to attract foreign investment, not for development, but simply as a holding service. By these means major corporations and wealthy individuals were able to avoid taxes and other irksome charges. This, in turn, has knock-on effects: tax takes fall and the money to run essential public services runs low. The tax burden is shifted from capital to land, which is of course completely immobile, and labour, which is a far more problematic a thing to move around than is money.

The globalisation of finance and the growing power of financial markets goes a long way to explain the ascendancy of the neoliberal economic philosophy. Finance capital represents a sort of footloose wealth, waiting to be invested in whatever offers the highest return. It is removed from the process of production in a way that manufacturing and distribution are not. A factory may move, but it must be somewhere. Finance capital is homeless, rootless, and, to a greater extent than ever, almost infinitely mobile. To close a factory and open another one elsewhere is an expensive process which may be made uncertain by direct resistance from the workforce, mandatory social obligations on employers making mass redundancies, and a host of other factors which can disrupt or delay the relocation. Investment capital can be moved with a couple of keystrokes or a terse phone call. The end result may be disruptive of people's lives, destroying livelihoods and devastating towns, regions, even countries; but the victims will never know who is responsible. It is the difference between bayoneting a man into whose eyes you can look and pressing a button that fires a missile that kills people a thousand miles away.

The concept of globalisation rests to a great extent on the idea that the amount and rapidity of movement of capital, of goods, and also of production, technology, ideas, worldviews and of people – not merely in their social role as 'labour' but also as tourists, scientists and intellectuals collaborating across borders and oceans, entertainers, and in a host of other functions – is now so great that it has transformed the world. And this transformation is visible not only in everyday life, but in a whole new set of institutions, or the reform of existing institutions so that they serve a particular end. The end result is the weakening of the nation state in favour of transnational corporations and international financial institutions.

Again, we must ask how accurate this assessment is, how different the world is from what went before. In the 19th century, capital and goods flowed between countries subordinated by imperial conquest – in Africa and Asia in particular – and those which had done the conquering, the imperial powers of Europe great and small. In modern times, the flow continues to be conditioned by unequal relationships. Though the countries of Africa and Asia are for the most part politically independent, their subordination is ensured by other means. Quite simply, as long as the gap in wealth between North and South remains so great, it is difficult to see how this could be changed.

Britain, the USA and the other industrialised or industrialising powers used their dominant position in the late 19th and early 20th centuries to create a global division of labour still recognisable in our own time. They did not want to create competitors, so refrained from encouraging industrialisation. What they wanted were cheap raw materials and cheap food, enabling them to keep production costs low at home. The kinds of development they encouraged, permitted and financed therefore tended to be in the extractive industries and agriculture. The goods that British people would have most readily associated with the Empire before the Second World War were farm products such as tea, chocolate, bananas and other tropical and subtropical fruit and, at least for those who worked in certain industries, mined metals

34

such as copper and gold. Long after the dismantling of the formal empire, such products continue to characterise the type of goods flowing from South to North though, as noted earlier, manufacturing has begun to play a more significant role. In the past, the cost of transport more than outweighed savings through cheap labour and low production costs. Now this is no longer the case, and investors can see a bigger return by putting their money into countries with extremely low wage rates.

Aid is one device for maintaining the subordination of poorer countries. Much of it is given on condition that it will be spent, in part, on goods and services produced by the donor country, or to encourage favourable investment conditions, trade privileges and so on. Aid can be used, in effect, to buy a way into a domestic market, to demand access to raw materials, to force weakening of laws protecting labour or the environment, to tailor, in short, local economies to the needs of the rich donor country. In other words, it helps achieve what imperialism achieved in the less civilised world of Victorian times. Third World governments accept it either out of desperation, or because they are run by people whose interests are closer to those of foreign investors and aid agencies than they are to those of their own poorer compatriots.

Much of this aid is channelled through Non-Governmental Organisations (NGOs). At the end of the 1990s, there were 50,000 organisations classed under this heading and operating in developing countries, ranging from giants such as Oxfam and Caritas to small, locally-based groups. The popular idea of such organisations is that they collect money direct from sympathetic members of the public and use this to finance their activities. In fact, NGOs receive a total of over $10 billion per annum in funding from government agencies in the developed world, from the European Union, international financial institutions (IFIs) and from governments in the countries in which they are operating. [5]

Globalisation, then, is scarcely a new phenomenon, though the modern version differs in many respects from its predecessors. In place of imperial decrees, we have structural adjustment programmes. Where District Commissioners once carried the White Man's Burden, economists from the IMF complain wearily of corruption and profligacy. And where once you had missionaries can now be found NGO fieldworkers, struggling to mitigate the effects of the economic behaviour of the governments that fund them.

Notes

1. *International Labour Organisation, World Employment, 1996* (ILO, 1996)
2. Susan George, interview in *New Scientist*, 27 April 2002, attributes this estimate to the International Labour Organisation.
3. *Financial Times*, 14 November 2001
4. 'Globalization: The Facts,' *New Internationalist*, Issue 296, at < http://www.newint.org/issue296/facts.html >
5. James Petras and Henry Veltmeyer, *Globalization Unmasked* (Zed Books, 2001)

3: Winners And Losers

'...all the evidence indicates that the winners could compensate
the losers and still come out ahead.'

George Soros [1]

For capital to be as mobile as possible, it is not enough to remove controls, or to develop efficient means of shifting cash over large distances. The goal of capital mobility also has enormous implications for policy, for how countries are run. Privatisation, for example, is essential to globalisation because it enables wealth to be transferred from one country to another, even when that wealth is produced by service activities which are essentially local in nature.

Privatisation has occurred not only in the wealthy metropolitan countries of the North, but in the Third World. There, in particular, the repatriation of profit and the prioritisation of shareholders' interests over those of service-users themselves have transformed the financial relationship between rich and poor nations. Until very recently infrastructure projects and other spending by Third World governments was financed through huge loans, loans which have led to the debt crisis which now faces many developing countries. In the last three decades, however, this has largely given way to direct investment by corporate finance, to what is called Foreign Direct Investment (FDI). Much of this FDI has been spent on privatisation. This has increased the vulnerability of developing countries, leading to a wave of financial crises in Latin America and the Far East.

The wave of privatisation which has characterised the last two decades is part of a contradictory process through which western TNCs are seeking to maintain and enhance their control of the international economy. Whilst US corporations are far more interested now than they were at any time in the past in developing markets beyond their country's borders, technological changes are enabling them to erode their dependence on the Third World as a source of raw materials. It is not that new domestic sources of necessary primary products have been discovered. Instead, what has happened is that raw materials themselves as an element in the value of the final product have diminished in importance.

Consider the actual value of, for example, a computer. Its case, the electronic circuitry, microchips, the whole (to most of us) mysterious and magical bag of tricks would be worth very little if its value were measured solely by the raw materials it contains. The major component of its value is neither raw materials nor the labour required to transform them into a useful (if maddening) object. What costs in that computer is rather the ingenuity which lies behind its development, and whilst no section of the human race has a monopoly on this quality, those with access to relatively well-funded education systems in countries where computers are familiar, everyday objects, will clearly enjoy an advantage.

The increasing domination of the international economy by TNCs based in the North, whose shareholders are predominantly also from the North, is one factor ensuring that money increasingly tends to flow from poorer to richer. In 1999, 244 of the top 500 companies in the world were based in the United States, 143 in Europe and 46 in Japan. During the 1990s, moreover, the threat to western domination from the Far East, if threat there had been, was largely neutralised through the assimilation of Japanese, Korean and other oriental TNCs. Of the top twenty-five firms, each of whose capitalisation exceeded $86 billion, only 4% were Japanese, and no others were based outside the two metropolitan areas of western Europe and the United States. [2] Furthermore, US domination is not confined to one area of the economy, however broadly defined. The world's two top firms are the high technology leaders Microsoft and the massively varied manufacturing empire of General Electric. US brand leaders top the pile in sportswear, soft drinks, tobacco, fast food and numerous other sectors.

When wages are low and corporate taxes are low, a relatively small proportion of the wealth generated by TNC subsidiaries remains in the countries where it is produced. This is a major factor contributing to a widening gap between rich and poor. The United Nations Development Programme has calculated that in 1980 the world's richest fifth commanded 11 times the wealth enjoyed by its poorest. By 1992, the ratio had grown to 17.[3]

Pro-globalisation economists argue that because liberalisation promotes economic growth, it will ultimately benefit everyone. It is, in leading businessman Henry Paulson's words, 'an essential part of the solution to world poverty,' and there is 'a close correlation... between the level of foreign direct investment in a country and its citizens' economic well-being.' [4] If benefits are unevenly spread or resources squandered, this is the fault of governments and not of corporations, the IMF or the WTO.

Paulson's argument seems difficult to square with the actual experience of developing countries. This is not to deny that governments have indeed been guilty of squandering the wealth their citizens' hard work has produced, of wasting foreign aid and, in the case of an unsavoury array of dictators, simply stealing it and salting it away in western bank accounts. In a few cases, state-owned enterprises have been little more than ways of channelling wealth into the foreign bank accounts of dictators and their henchmen, and this has led in some countries to widespread support for privatisation.

'Good government,' or 'governance' (a broader concept which includes administrative institutions at all levels) is nowadays in an increasing number of cases made a precondition of the award of loans or grants. Taxpayers in the developed countries are generally sympathetic to such ideas, feeling that whilst they are prepared to help the needy, much of the aid given does not reach the intended beneficiary.

Paulson gives a number of criteria for 'good government.' Such a government would bring about 'stability' through 'commitment to the rule of law and economic progress for all, through empowered people and an educated workforce.' [5] The first of these concepts is too vague and malleable to be of much use as a measuring stick. One person's 'stability' is another's stagnation. China has shown remarkable stability since emerging from the troubled period of the Cultural Revolution, yet few argue that it is a model to be emulated, and it is unlikely that Henry Paulson counts himself among that few. Moreover, the closer China comes to following the type of economics favoured by neoliberal reformers, the less 'stable' it becomes. In fact, as it plugs into the global economy, a process exemplified by its recent accession to the WTO, the People's Republic is beginning to suffer from the same kinds of problem experienced elsewhere in developing countries during periods of rapid growth and economic opening: the sudden enriching of small but visible sections of the population generating discontent amongst everyone else; surplus labour from the countryside flooding into already overstretched cities; and a rapid spread of the diseases of affluence rather than of its benefits, with prostitution, drug abuse, petty crime and corruption enjoying greater visibility than the government's attempts to increase the standard of living for the masses through such measures as improved sanitation.

China's people are scarcely 'empowered,' but whether they have any less control over their rulers than do the inhabitants of a nominal democracy such as the Philippines or Indonesia is doubtful. These two countries, with their bewildering array of parties and more or less open vote-selling and general corruption, clearly demonstrate that the creation of nominally parliamentary institutions is no guarantee of popular empowerment. On the other hand, the sustained economic success of Singapore and South Korea, with their dictatorial systems hidden behind elections which are little more than shams, calls into question the whole idea that popular democracy is essential to economic success. It is also curious to recall that the ideas of neoliberalism were first applied in Chile, and that this followed a US-backed military coup which abolished democratic institutions and established the dictatorship of Auguste Pinochet. It seems much more likely that causation moves in the other direction: once people have time and resources beyond what are needed for the basic essentials, they begin to organise to improve their lot.

Structural Adjustment Programmes, which invariably involve deregulation, liberalisation and privatisation, lead to neglect of the kind of long-term investment needed to produce Paulson's other cornerstone of prosperity, 'an educated workforce.' In fact, it is inputs such as those needed to build, staff and run effective universities, schools, training colleges and kindergartens that tend to be the first to go when IMF spending constraints are imposed.

Pro-globalisation theorists and their opponents can invariably cite statistics which appear to back up their arguments. One problem is that they do not always share the same concerns, and so what the two groups are saying may well, in its own terms, be true, even when their interpretation and conclusions are wildly at odds.

Take the rather fundamental question of whether a country is becoming more, or less, prosperous. Globalisers can point to sometimes impressive increases in GDP which have followed liberalisation. Their opponents do not necessarily question the figures directly, arguing instead that measuring development by GNP has never been a fully satisfactory method. The idea that this measure of aggregate wealth gives a good guide to reality has in recent times, moreover, been called increasingly into question amongst an ever-wider group of economists and political thinkers.

To see the limitations of GDP as an accurate measuring rod, imagine a country where few people own cars and travel over any distance is invariably by train. The train system is a bit ramshackle but basically functioning. It takes six hours to travel the 200 kilometres between the country's two main population centres. Then oil is discovered and a reasonably egalitarian economic policy ensures that most people in the country become substantially better off. In addition, oil becomes cheaper and more plentiful. Car manufacturers know a good market when they see one, so they promote an affordable range of vehicles and the thing to own becomes a car. The trains are now so poorly used that services become erratic or cease to function. For a while, the better off people who are the first to be able to afford cars are winning. They can now get between the two cities in three hours, half the time it took them by train. Gradually, however, as more and more people buy cars, journey times prolong and eventually reach the same length as they were when undertaken by train. What's more, productive land, biodiversity and beautiful scenery all disappear under a new network of roads. Nobody has gained very much, and things have been lost. Yet GDP has risen immensely as people spend enhanced incomes on buying cars and maintaining them, and the country invests its oil wealth in roads.

Far from being a fanciful example, this is in fact what has happened, to one degree or another, and of course with huge variations of detail, in every developed, and some developing, economies since the Second World War. And transport is only one sector in which this process is visible.

GDP measures aggregate quantities of goods and services, whatever the real value of those goods and services may be. It makes no judgement of value beyond the market, and views £1,000's worth of effective medical care as worth no more nor less than £1,000's worth of video games, cigarettes, guns or Christmas crackers.

For this reason, numerous individuals and organisations have suggested different ways of measuring economic well-being, or the lack of it. The United Nations Development Programme, for example, publishes an annual Human Development Index based on a range of indicators including levels of literacy, nutrition, health and gender equality, and takes into account the environmental and social cost of any economic activity. Alternatively, a single indicator may be used. Maternal and infant mortality are popular: clearly, a society which cannot successfully propagate its young is in trouble. On this measure, little progress has been made anywhere in the last two decades, during which GNP-based statistics would have us believe that the world has become more and more prosperous, albeit unevenly. In 1997, in fact, almost half of the world was experiencing an increase in maternal mortality, while less than a quarter was making significant progress. [6] Even the vanguard institutions of globalisation, the World Bank and IMF, accept that some parts of the world have gone backwards rather than making progress towards a more prosperous future. The World Bank estimates that real incomes per head in sub-Saharan Africa have fallen by a quarter since 1987. [7] Rather than blaming globalisation, however, the Bank and the Fund prescribe stronger doses of the same medicine, coupled with improvements in 'governance' to enable planned reforms to be implemented.

Anti-globalisers argue that real social conditions in the world are regressing, that access to healthcare, for example, is becoming more restrictive, that job security is diminishing and working conditions deteriorating almost

41

everywhere, that even retirement ages are being pushed back and inclusive pension schemes being replaced by privately run targeted pensions for those who can afford them. Countering this, World Bank economists assert that 'the developing countries that have integrated most strongly into the global economy in the past two decades have grown rapidly and reduced poverty.' Developing countries defined as 'globalisers' have grown 'at about 3.5 per cent per capita in the 1990s, compared to 2 per cent in rich countries and negative growth in the rest of the developing world.' [8]

One problem with such an analysis is that it takes us right back to a reliance on the flawed indicator of GDP, or growth in per capita wealth. Some values are quantifiable, others not. An urban factory worker with an income of $2,000 per year is clearly better off than a farmer on an income of $500 per year. If she has no access to food other than by purchasing it, her every trip to the market will add to GDP. If she has enough money left after feeding, housing and clothing herself and her family then she may treat herself to a television, or reduce the time she has to spend getting to work by investing in a motor scooter. Her brother who stays on his farm will not be able to afford such things. However, he and his family may live in an easily-maintained traditional house, which they have owned for generations. If he wants to watch TV, perhaps he will gather with others in a village cafe. He does not need a motor scooter to reach his fields or the nearby village. He may not have any money left after laying out for those necessities he cannot grow, but perhaps there are things which cost nothing which he values or enjoys.

This is not to idealise rural life over that of the city. For poor people, both have their hazards and hardships, and both their compensations. Some urban pleasures are also free for all, or affordable even to the poor. It is merely to point out that some values are quantifiable and some are intangible, which distorts the picture. Changing patterns of trade with their accompanying transformations of economies in countries rich and poor, the increasing concentration of land ownership, the destruction of traditional practices and the local enterprises which depended upon them, have all had adverse affects for some groups of people. Global unemployment has risen hugely, yet a country where a quarter of the population is permanently unemployed or underemployed will be richer than one where everyone is in work, provided the total value of what is produced and consumed in the latter country is greater.

If you go out into your yard at dawn, pick up an egg that was laid by a chicken you inherited as part of your family's modest estate, take it into your house, boil it on a fire burning wood you gathered the previous day in a nearby forest, you add nothing to GDP. If you walk down to where that forest used to be and buy yourself an Egg McMuffin, your country just grew richer.

The division of opinion regarding globalisation is often presented by anti-globalisers as pitting rich against poor, strong against powerful. In reality, and unsurprisingly, things are a little more complicated than that. Whilst powerful states tend to be enthusiastic globalisers, there are influential forces within them which are more equivocal. Even in the United States can be seen the persistence of an isolationism which was once its dominant ideology, not so much America first as America first, middle and last. This tendency has expressions on both the left of the spectrum, amongst workers fearing that their jobs will be exported to low-wage countries, and on the right, where politicians often seem motivated by the idea that everyone envies and hates the US for its success and wealth, an idea given a powerful boost by the events of September 11th 2001. In France, anxiety about globalisation often takes cultural forms: pop radio stations forced to give a certain proportion of their air time to home-grown products; an aggressive pursuit of a world free from fizzy wine that has the temerity to call itself Champagne; a far-right nationalist wins almost 17% of Presidential votes; militant farmers tear down a McDonald's because they see it as a threat, not so much to their livelihoods but to the whole range of traditions and practices which in their view add up to being French. Within the European Union, in fact, we find a whole gamut of attitudes, from the almost messianic globalising of the British or Dutch governments to the equivocation of countries as different as Denmark and Greece – different, but united in the value they place on an independence which has been breached many times, and most recently within the memories of the oldest of their citizens.

In the Third World, it is generally the case that elites who stand to benefit from the financial opportunities globalisation brings are likely to be the most enthusiastic about the process. However, here too we find a variety of approaches. Some countries' ruling groups have rejected globalisation: one might include Cuba and North Korea, the former subject to a forty-year US blockade which makes any possibility of a normalisation of trade impossible, the latter ruled by extreme isolationists. In addition, in recent times, Venezuela, Malaysia, a number of Arab countries, Iran and a handful of others have attempted to develop their economies in defiance of the dictate of IMF, WTO and World Bank. Each has, however, had to pay a considerable price for this. In their different ways China and India have attempted to use their very large populations almost as negotiating tools: seen, rightly or wrongly, as potentially huge and valuable markets, they have been able, though gradually adjusting to the demands of globalisation, to extract concessions, negotiate compromises, preserve some of what they wish to preserve. In such matters vested interests exist on both sides: the Chinese Communist Party, in particular, is attempting to preside over the reintroduction of a market economy, with all the potential upheaval that brings, whilst remaining firmly in the driving seat. In other countries the educated, the rich and the privileged are most likely to be found on the pro-globalisation side of the fence, but not always. Countries which have had bloated state bureaucracies also produce elites with a vested interest in maintaining the old ways of doing things. In general, bankers and others who control finance capital are enthusiasts, as are those who make a living, or a fortune, from trading goods and services across borders. Less enthusiastic are the owners and managers of small and medium-sized enterprises whose localised markets may be threatened by the lowering of tariffs and the removal of other barriers to trade, and corrupt officials whose income depends on creaming off income from state-owned enterprises.

At the other end of the socio-economic scale, it is difficult to find working people, small farmers or others who must rely on their own labour to survive who are not at least wary of globalisation – though they have never heard what is happening called by that term. Even if the now mainstream view of the untold virtues of free trade turns out to be correct, the initial impact of deregulation has been difficult for small farmers serving local markets, where protectionist measures have been eroded or discarded, opening the way to cheap foreign imports.

In fact, it is scarcely accurate to blame the whole of this on 'free trade,' because while insisting on the lowering or removal of import restrictions both the European Union and the United States subsidise their own food exports, benefiting farmers at home whilst in some cases devastating producers in developing countries. A recent Oxfam report, for example, concluded that the EU was guilty of gross protectionism at the expense of poor countries. Worse, subsidies aimed at lowering the export price of grain have resulted in greater concentration of land ownership and depopulation of the countryside as small farmers are forced to sell up and move off the land and flood into the city. Those poor farmers who choose, or are able, to remain in the countryside, are increasingly reduced to wage labour, forced to exchange the perhaps precarious but familiar and often culturally valued status of farmer-proprietor for the still more precarious and, for many, unfamiliar and even humiliating position of day labourer. [9]

Wage earners in both developed and developing countries may value some of the cultural aspects of globalisation, but for these they must pay dearly, with the constant menace of plant relocation, and a sort of 'race to the bottom' where countries compete to see who can provide the best environment for corporate business, eroding rights, conditions, wages, pensions and other benefits. Nevertheless, not all working people regard globalisation as menacing to their well-being. Those in export industries are likely to see immediate and tangible benefits in, for example, the opening up of new markets. Others, employed in the sort of public services that have come under pressure as states seek to reduce their spending, or those who work in industries likely to suffer most from increased foreign imports, are less likely to view the process positively. This does not, however, always result in their embracing more radical social and political perspectives. On the contrary, the very nature of globalisation encourages in some cases a xenophobic response. Not only left-wing leaders like José Bové have sought to defend French traditions. The same rallying cry, manipulated to take in an anti-immigration message, can be heard on the lips of Jean-Marie Le Pen, Jorgen Haider and others of the far right. In the United States, the decline of the auto industry has provoked periodic outbursts of anti-Japanese feeling.

John Kay has written that the 'principal victims of globalisation are companies, activities and individuals in rich countries with strong historic positions but no competitive advantages: US car workers, Bethlehem Steel, Sabena.' [10] Even if Kay overstates his case, ignores the many other victims of the process – not to mention the blamelessness of even these victims – it is true that these groups have suffered. Their response will tend to differ greatly according to their own traditions, to what might be called the political culture in which they live. The Belgian employees of Sabena reached out to others, both inside and outside their country, for solidarity and support. US steel workers also have a militant history but they operate in a country where such traditions have never been as strong as they are in Europe, and where they are now critically weakened. They therefore appealed to a right wing president, George W. Bush, to take measures which would protect their jobs but only at the expense of those of workers elsewhere: in this case, moreover, not in Vietnam or Indonesia but in The Netherlands and Britain. In the glorious age of free trade triumphant, labour militants demanded an old-fashioned protectionist response to hard times.

They demanded it, moreover, of a President whose flag is nailed firmly to the mast of the globalisers' ship. They got their tariffs.

Notes

1. George Soros, *George Soros On Globalization* (Perseus Books Public Affairs, 2002)
2. *Financial Times*, 28 January 1999
3. United Nations Development Programme, Human Development: Reports 1992 (New York & Oxford: Oxford University Press, 1992)
4. Henry Paulson, 'The Gospel Of Globalisation,' *Financial Times*, 12 November 2001
5. Henry Paulson, 'The Gospel Of Globalisation,' *Financial Times*, 12 November 2001
6. Instituto del Tercer Mundo, Uraguay, Social Watch, No 1, 1997
7. World Bank World Development Report, 2000-2001
8. Paul Collier and David R. Dollar in a letter to the *Financial Times*, 2 January 2002
9. Oxfam, *Rigged Rules And Double Standards: Trade, Globalisation And The Fight Against Poverty* (Oxfam, 2002) available at http://www.maketrade-fair.org/stylesheet.asp
10. John Kay, 'Globalisation's Paradox,' *Financial Times*, 12 November 2001

4: Managing Globalisation

'What we have now is a slow motion coup d'état, a low intensity war waged to redefine free society – democracy and its non-commercial health, safety and other protections – as subordinate to the dictates of international trade – i.e. big business über alles.'

Ralph Nader [1]

In spite of claims that globalisation is somehow inevitable, it could not occur in its present form without the deliberate intervention of powerful people organised into powerful transnational institutions. In this chapter, I will try to define and clarify the roles of the most important of these: the World Bank, which presides over development, part-finances actual practical projects and plays a role in encouraging free trade; the International Monetary Fund (IMF), which loans money to countries experiencing difficulties and uses the power this role gives it to promote a particular monetary orthodoxy; the World Trade Organisation (WTO), which fixes the rules of trade and ensures that countries do not seek an unfair advantage, though it is accused of doing so in a way that benefits the richest and most powerful countries, and at the expense of environmental and social considerations; and a host of other bodies which, either on the global level (the G7 and G8, the Trilateral Commission, the World Economic Forum) or regionally (the EU, NAFTA) pursue the same goals through the same orthodoxy. Standing behind these institutions are an estimated 37,000 firms that could be classed as Transnational Corporations (TNCs).

The World Trade Organisation (WTO)

Towards the end of the Second World War a group of high-ranking government officials, politicians, bankers, economists and other experts from the Allied countries gathered at a hotel in Bretton Woods, New Hampshire. Their purpose was to discuss an institutional framework which would enable the world to be reconstructed, and in a way which would reduce inequalities whilst leaving the market economy intact. The result was a new structure for global finance based on the IMF and World Bank, both of which functioned successfully as important elements in that reconstruction.

Trade proved more problematic. Even traditionally isolationist elements on the American right could live with the institutionalisation of development which the two great International Financial Institutions (IFIs) represented. In a ravaged world, it made sense and would, it was argued, prevent the United States from having to bear a disproportionate amount of the burden. Trade, on the other hand, was a minor player in America's vision of the post-war world, and an institution which was designed to prevent states from seeking an unfair advantage over their rivals was no part of that vision at all. Advantages, unfair or not, were what the US had in abundance and it aimed to hang on to them.

This deadly mixture of indifference and hostility was enough to kill off plans for an International Trade Organisation (ITO). Instead, a much more limited agreement, the General Agreement on Tariffs and Trade, set in motion a stop-go liberalisation. The WTO did not emerge until 1994. With over 140 members, and around a further thirty applicants, it now accounts for over 97% of world trade.[2] Its purpose is to establish universally recognised rules governing trade between nations. The potential benefits of such a project are clear. An effective WTO would benefit both producers and consumers by smoothing out the vagaries and uncertainties of trade, increasing market access and competition, improving security of supply, guaranteeing safety and quality. The WTO's rules are the result of negotiations between the members. The current set were the outcome of the 1986–94 Uruguay Round negotiations which led to its establishment. At Doha in the Gulf State of Oman in October, 2001, member states succeeded where the previous WTO meeting, in Seattle two years earlier had failed, instigating a new round of trade negotiations which will eventually result in a further revision of the GATT.

The Uruguay Round also created new rules for dealing with trade in services, relevant aspects of intellectual property, dispute settlement and trade policy reviews. Through these agreements, WTO members are obliged to follow what is ostensibly a non-discriminatory trading system that spells out their rights and their obligations. Each country receives guarantees that its exports will be treated fairly and consistently in other countries' markets. Each promises to do the same for imports into its own market.

Those who defend the WTO-based system would point out that all of its agreements contain special provisions relating to poorer member states. Developing countries are generally given more time to implement agreements and commitments, for example, and measures are included whose aim is to increase their trading opportunities. They are also given support in creating the facilities necessary for WTO participation, such as presenting their case in disputes, or implementing technical standards.

The 2001 Ministerial Conference in Doha, moreover, paid special attention to the needs of developing countries, partly as a response to the rising tide of criticism which had first made itself spectacularly visible at Seattle two years earlier. It was before that, however, in 1997, that the WTO established what it calls an 'integrated framework' involving six separate intergovernmental agencies, with the aim of helping the poorest countries, the so-called least-developed countries (LDCs) to increase their capacity to trade.

So, given this apparently helpful attitude, what precisely is supposed to be the problem?

Trade governed by an equitable system could arguably provide a sound basis for a system of international relations, and the extension from bilateral to multilateral agreements is a logical and potentially positive step. However, while most WTO decisions are, on paper, arrived at through consensus among all member countries, that consensus tends to reflect the will of the powerful. The United States and other powerful nations and blocs of the developed world have tailored the system to their own needs, using it, for example, to put pressure on poorer countries to get rid of subsidies and trade barriers, whilst at the same time refusing to remove their own.

True, the WTO works to a transparent rule book and the rules apply equally to everyone. Yet if those rules have been written to reinforce the power of the already strong, their equal enforcement does not mean that the system is fair. It is as if basketball had been invented by the tallest tribe in the forest, who then challenged their pigmy neighbours to a game. The rules would, of course, be the same for both sides.

The basic assumption is that free trade under a market system is the ideal. This hugely narrows the possible range of action of democratically elected governments. Of course, you may subsidise that shipyard to keep people in work; you can exclude Genetically Modified Organisms (GMOs) because your people don't want to eat them; you can keep those furs out because the traps their original owners were caught in are judged to be cruel and inhumane punishment for the crime of being fluffy. It's just that if you do, the WTO might take action against you on behalf of the aggrieved importer, up to and including suspending or expelling you, in which case hardly anyone will trade with you any more.

This is what makes the WTO such a powerful instrument of globalisation. The multilateral trading system imposes a particular view of correct commercial policy on everyone. In so doing it homogenises the world, narrowing political debate, eroding cultural variety and allowing certain big brands to force others from the market. At the same time, by insisting that trade must take precedence in most cases over social and environmental considerations, it forces the whole world to accept the skewed priorities of the most powerful trading nations.

Opposition from third world governments and from activists everywhere has produced a certain caution in recent times, with senior WTO officials stressing the fact that countries do have the right to exclude goods and other items of trade on a range of social and environmental grounds. They can do so, however, only with the WTO's permission, because it is the Organisation which must adjudicate in disputes between nations. Moreover, despite the rejection of the Multilateral Agreement on Investments (MAI), which would have denied to governments a range of powers needed to control the activities of TNCs on their territory, attempts continue to extend the principle of trade-at-all-costs further into the realm of financial and other services.

In the WTO worldview, small farmers whose yield per hectare is lower than that of great plantations or mono-cultural near-deserts are deemed 'less efficient,' even if whole valued ways of life and landscapes hundreds or thousands of years old depend upon their survival. Food security through import substitution is no kind of goal for a 'modern' government, because interdependence amongst nations is always a good thing and should be maximised. Nationalisation and other forms of public ownership are not actually outlawed, but they are regarded as deeply suspect forms of subsidy disguised under outdated ideological baggage. Consumers, as individuals, can presumably always choose not to buy Japanese products because they don't approve of whaling, or Pakistani goods because of the persecution of religious minorities, or Turkish goods because of that country's illegal occupation of Cyprus or repressive behaviour towards Kurds. Their elected representatives, however, who in a democracy are supposed to embody and make more effective the people's will, may not take any of these actions. They must sign up to the whole WTO rulebook, surrender to the power of its decision-making bodies, or find themselves ostracised.

The International Monetary Fund

Unlike the WTO the IMF saw the light of day before the smell of cordite had passed from the battlefields of Europe and Asia. Two days after Christmas, 1945, the first twenty-nine countries signed the IMF Articles of Agreement and the Fund did its first real business just over a year later, on 1 March 1947. More than half a century on, membership has grown to include 183 countries.

The principle motive behind the establishment of the IMF was a desire to promote international monetary cooperation as a basis of the kind of stability which had been so lacking in the years leading up to the War. Such cooperation, it was hoped and believed, would provide a firm basis for the expansion and balanced growth of trade, helping to avoid financial crises brought about by lopsided national balance sheets, uncoordinated monetary policies and inefficient distribution of capital.

At least since the 1970s, however, this has meant in practice the imposition of monetary orthodoxy. The Fund appraises its members' exchange rate policies within the framework of a comprehensive analysis of the general economic situation; it holds consultations with individual countries; and in response to difficulties it may prescribe reforms, often grouped together as Structural Adjustment Programmes (SAPs). The overall, stated aim is to encourage policies which the Fund believes lead to stable exchange rates, which it in turn sees as a cornerstone of global prosperity. The IMF's policies are not, however, determined democratically, as the size of a member's vote is determined by the size of its net contribution, so that those who put most in have most votes, and those which take most out the least. The Group of 7 (commonly known as G7 and comprising the US, the UK, Japan, Germany, France, Canada and Italy) holds over 40% of the votes on the IMF boards.

Why do poorer countries put up with this, and why do they follow the Fund's edicts, even though these generally involve cutbacks in public spending which almost invariably lead to unrest and worse? The answer is that financial assistance is typically offered by the IMF when it is unavailable elsewhere, which means that it tends to be available to those seeking their way out of a tight corner. And it comes attached to strings so thick and knotty that they have choked many a government which has tried to swallow them.

Like the WTO, the IMF is an instrument of globalisation – of the particular kind of globalisation which we are seeing – because it operates from within a framework based on a 'one-size-fits-all' perspective. Whatever the question, the answer is free trade. Whatever the problem, the solution is structural adjustment. Moreover, structural adjustment always means the same thing: a reduced role for the state in the economy through privatisation and deregulation, reduced public spending, the opening up of markets, the encouragement of foreign direct investment and the establishment of a new, business-friendly economic framework designed to restore the confidence of investors. And investors, of course, especially foreign corporate investors, are notoriously averse to troublesome labour unions, irksome labour and environmental protection laws, expensive education systems and welfare states, and paying taxes.

As Britain, then Germany, then the US and other countries industrialised in the 19th century, they found eventually that a disciplined, efficient workforce capable of producing supervisory grade workers and craftspeople demanded the establishment of universal education. To one degree or another they learned the value of widely available and effective healthcare in reducing absenteeism and ensuring, when needed, a supply of men who were literally fighting fit. They learned, too, that workers given some sort of stake in the system were less likely to listen to those who sought capitalism's destruction.

The image presented by those who see globalisation as a positive and progressive development is one of a world where each country is given the chance to follow just this path. The result, some time in this century, would surely be a world in which everyone enjoyed the kind of prosperity, social security, democratic rights and freedoms, and level of material well-being commonplace in the wealthy west.

The problem is that the imperatives which transformed the lives of men, women and children in the wake of First World industrialisation are absent or weak in the developing countries of the early 21st century. For foreign investors, there are too many cheaper, simpler alternatives. Social peace can be guaranteed not by accommodating people's aspirations, but instead by increasing repression. Jobs requiring workers with some degree of education can be saved for the folks back home. Markets can be created not by improving poorer people's incomes, but by transforming consumerism into a virtual religion and concentrating on enhancing the wealth of those who already have it. In the 19th century, rich men with money to burn notoriously commissioned 'follies,' useless but amusing edifices which cost thousands of pounds each. Today, you can spend $18 million on a weekend in space.

The World Bank

Like the IMF, the World Bank was conceived at Bretton Woods and went to work almost immediately after the war ended, making its first loan – $250 million to France – in 1947.[3] Much of its activity since has been directed at similar scenarios of reconstruction following wars, natural disasters and other calamities. It has been active, for example, in recent years in: Bosnia, Kosovo and East Timor following armed conflict; East Asia to address the problems resulting from the financial crisis that engulfed the region; central America after the recent series of hurricanes and Turkey in the wake of its last major earthquake. Its ostensible primary aim, however, is poverty reduction, and not only in situations demanding crisis management. It likes to present itself as working 'in the field' and 'at the grass roots.' Though like the IMF it has its head office in Washington, 40% of its staff are based in recipient countries. Just as with the IMF, however, the G7 countries control 40% of the votes on the board.

Though it was founded as a unitary institution, the increasing size and complexity of its operations have led to its development into a group of five development institutions for which 'World Bank' remains a handy collective term. The Bank's worldview is precisely that of the IMF and WTO: it sees the route out of poverty, and therefore the way to fulfil its remit, as being a judicious mix of monetarist economics, large-scale infrastructure investments, social and economic policies designed to attract inward investment and the removal of barriers to trade of all kinds.

Unlike the IMF and WTO, however, the Bank is responsible for direct investment and can therefore determine which development projects are deemed worthy of support. The strategies of the two financial institutions are complementary, and can best be understood as a single project, aided by the WTO, to further globalisation.

The World Bank and IMF sometimes appear like the movie cliché of the good cop/bad cop duo. The World Bank announces itself as an institution whose goal is a world without poverty. The IMF seems less concerned with sugar-coating the pill. Yet the World Bank has a very poor record in relation to what might be called 'quality control': few of the mega-projects which it finances – typically dams, roads and power plants – can record any measurable impact they have made on levels of poverty, whilst they are often demonstrably responsible for environmental devastation and social dislocation.

Structural Adjustment Programmes

Conditions enforced by the IMF and World Bank in extending loans or part-financing projects typically force developing countries to introduce labour market reforms which reduce protection and security for workers. They usually, moreover, attempt to reorient economic activity towards export markets. This reduces balance of payments deficits, alleviating debt and, if successful, leads to a lowering of interest rates and other positive economic developments. On the other hand, crops and goods for export may be produced at the expense of commodities needed by poor domestic consumers, as in parts of East Africa where flowers and luxury fruits for the western European market have replaced staple crops and subsistence farmers have been driven off the land to become wage labourers in export-directed farms, market gardens and factories.

Around ninety countries have been subject to programmes which hand over a large degree of economic control to the IMF and/or the World Bank. [3] The chosen instrument of this control is the Structural Adjustment Programme (SAP). SAPs involve cuts in social and welfare spending, with the money saved going to repay external debt. Financial shortfalls can also be met by introducing fees for services (including schools) which were previously free at the point of delivery. Increased school fees lead, at best, to a two-tier system where the quality of what is on offer corresponds to the quantity of money in parents' wallets. The likely consequence is that some children will be withdrawn from school. The world being the way it is, it is often girls who are the first to be taken out.

Women are disproportionate sufferers from these policies at other stages of their lives. Higher fees for medical service mean less treatment, more suffering and needless deaths. It often falls to already overburdened women to make up for the lack of healthcare, providing nursing and traditional medicines for their families. And whilst men generally do not need healthcare unless and until they get sick or old, women's reproductive health demands the kind of attention which it is unlikely to receive in a fee-based system.

Government expenditure could in many cases be reduced by cutting or eliminating defence spending but the influence of powerful US and EU arms manufacturers closes this option off. Instead, the state is constrained to look for reductions in any and every other area of the budget. Staffing levels are cut, leading directly to unemployment and a reduction in extent and quality of public services, and to weaker enforcement of such measures as environmental and workplace health and safety regulations.

Although reducing demand for capital lowers external debt and can in theory lead to lower interest rates, the initial approach of almost all SAPs is to force them upwards. Higher interest rates, it is argued, lower inflation, attract inward investment and 'shake down' economies, forcing inefficient producers to give way to competitors with higher rates of productivity and profit. One result is that small farmers leave the land to swell the ranks of the urban unemployed, see their status transformed from proprietors to tenants or even debt peons, or are forced into cultivating more marginal lands which offer a lowered standard of living for a greater amount of work. With the most productive land reserved for cash crops for export, the use of marginal land for subsistence crops leads to soil erosion. National food security, no longer of course seen as a worthy goal, is undermined and eventually destroyed. The poor country then becomes wholly dependent on a trading system controlled by the G7.

Globalisation is, of course, about creating One World, where such old-fashioned and dangerous concepts as national sovereignty are eliminated, or at least transformed in meaning. Regulations governing foreign ownership of land and other resources, commonplace in Third World countries as well as the 'transition' economies of Eastern and Central Europe, are seen as xenophobic and anachronistic, and SAPs typically force their removal. The result is to make it easier for TNCs to install themselves, for foreign agri-business corporations to buy up swathes of land and, again, for well-established locally-owned farms and firms to find themselves suddenly deprived of markets, unable to compete with their more 'efficient' rivals. Coupled with privatisation, this leads to wealth being transferred from the people of a poor country to shareholders from rich countries. Unable to say, 'Thanks, but we don't really want to play this game,' poor countries often feel they have been left with no choice but to enter into it as enthusiastically as possible, competing with each other, through tax breaks, repressive labour policies, weak environmental regulations and so on, to attract TNCs and foreign investment in general.

These central features of all SAPs are backed by a selection from a host of other market-liberalisation measures: subsidies for staple foods and other necessities are removed; any assistance to subsistence or semi-subsistence farms is ended, or made conditional on their moving over to export crops.

Employment for the people of a country is typically transformed from a variety of occupations and economic relationships to one where most people are wage earners or members of wage earners' families and most rural inhabitants no longer own the land that they work. This increases the supply of potential wage labour and reduces its cost.

Such policies are almost universally unpopular, leading to short-term pain. This is supposedly in exchange for long-term gain, though there seems little or no evidence that austerity benefits anyone other than a small local elite and foreign TNCs. People might vote for such policies once, even twice, but after a while the promises of jam tomorrow begin to sound more and more unconvincing. The results of this are threatening to any possibility that truly democratic institutions can be maintained, enhanced or spread. Dictatorships are fine as long as they deliver the goods: democratic institutions are okay as long as they do not interfere.

The European Union

The European Union, like NAFTA, is a regional organisation which favours globalisation and which works to an agenda and on the basis of a philosophy similar to that of the IMF and WTO. By transferring major decision-making powers to unelected bodies – the European Central Bank (ECB), the European Commission, and the committees and other institutions which serve them – the EU demonstrates the same limited concept of democracy which is so pervasive amongst the partisans of the IMF and WTO.

Economic and Monetary Union effectively eliminates popular democracy as an element that influences macroeconomic policy. The ECB is constitutionally 'independent,' a positive-sounding word deliberately chosen to mask the fact that what it is 'independent' of is the electorate and the politicians they choose to run their countries' affairs. Even the Council of Ministers, which is made up of men and women answerable to elected parliaments, meets behind closed doors and refuses to publish minutes or roll-call votes.

The EU shares with the global institutions discussed above a belief in technocracy, that experts are the best people to run things and that, for example, ordinary people and the non-experts they insist on elevating to power cannot be trusted to run the economy. Such matters must be left to specialists, to bankers. Of course, it is hard to understand the arcane workings of the economy, but no more difficult than it is to understand, say, molecular biology. Does that mean that we must leave decisions about food safety to scientists, that they have no obligation to listen to the people? Of course not: the true order of responsibility is that scientists, economists and other experts are, in a democracy, obliged to explain their plans in ways that the rest of us can understand, then step back while we consider them and, through the ballot box, free assemblies and a free press, make our views heard, 'views' that should be regarded as sovereign.

As with the WTO, the European Union takes control of the law out of the hands of elected governments. Once, all decisions taken by the EEC had to be unanimous. Now, the system of Qualified Majority Voting (QMV), which is extended with every revision of the EU Treaty, means that laws can be imposed on people against their express wishes and over the heads of their elected representatives. All of this is done in the name of 'efficiency.' It is true that unanimity is difficult to achieve and that QMV makes things bowl along faster. Yet democracy has always had this drawback. Dictatorships, by this measure, are the most efficient systems of all.

The Union's role in globalisation can be seen by its policies and programmes. The policies pursued by member state governments are increasingly constrained by EU rules which oblige them to impose a 'free market' logic on ever-broader areas of the economy.

Enlargement has become more a way of enforcing the EU's version of this free market on Central and Eastern Europe than any kind of move towards a unified continent of peace and prosperity. The Common Foreign and Security Policy (CFSP) is designed to allow the establishment of an EU armed force and promote a competitive arms industry, not to reduce international tensions that lead to war. Decisions on internal security are, especially since September 11, taken in an atmosphere of secrecy and mistrust, branding peaceful demonstrators as potential terrorists. Agricultural policy follows the wishes of the biggest farmers and agribusiness corporations; transport policy is hugely influenced by the powerful road lobby; and the environment, to which both of these areas of policy are enormously damaging, is protected by EU laws invariably watered down under pressure from corporate lobbyists, often to the point where they are ineffective or inadequate. Finally, the Maastricht Treaty's convergence criteria for admission to the single currency and the rules for participation bear an uncanny resemblance to the IMF's Structural Adjustment Programmes, obliging member states to respect very narrow, arbitrarily established limits on public borrowing and debt, to submit to a common interest rate which may be utterly inimical to their actual needs and to prioritise low inflation as a policy target: to follow, in other words, a particular idea of fiscal prudence. You may think these are a fine set of rules. If you do not, however, forget it: no one is ever going to ask your opinion, unless, of course, you work in a senior position at the European Central Bank.

There are those who argue that a powerful bloc of European nations could help to protect us from the undesirable aspects of globalisation, that, apart from the US and perhaps a handful of other rich, powerful countries, single nations can no longer exercise any real power in the world. This is no doubt true, but the EU does not fit the bill, unless you believe that, as in wartime, the crisis we face is so great that democratic freedoms must be sacrificed. Truly democratic international institutions would enable cooperation to take place between states and peoples while allowing electorates to control, or at least influence, the decisions of those they elect. The existing, globalising European Union stands in the way of this.

NATO And The New World Order

It may surprise some to see NATO listed as an instrument of globalisation. After all, if you don't obey WTO orders then the country that brought the complaint against you is allowed to take various retaliatory measures, but so far these have stopped mercifully short of permission to bomb the offender's major cities.

True, NATO, or the United States and allies, has in recent years launched military actions against Yugoslavia, Iraq, Sudan, Somalia and Afghanistan. Weren't these actions, however, designed to prevent human rights abuses, to halt and punish unprovoked invasions of neighbouring countries, or combat terrorism?

Certainly, these motives were involved. However, in each case other countries have committed similar actions and gone unpunished: the Soviet Union, Indonesia, Israel, India and Turkey have, in the last few decades, all invaded neighbouring countries without any armed response from what is now called the 'international community.' The Turkish state routinely uses torture and terror against those it sees as its enemies, including the Kurdish minority. And post-Soviet Russia has used extremes of military repression to suppress rebellion in Chechenya.

It is hard not to conclude that, to avoid provoking an unfriendly visit from the US Air Force, it is more important to play the globalisers' game than it is to improve your human rights record or consign military aggression against neighbours to the past. What the pariah states – Libya, North Korea, Iraq, Iran, Cuba and, until recently, Serbia/Yugoslavia – have in common may include a repressive government, but if this is the case they share this with many countries which go unpunished. What they also have in common is the pursuit of an independent economic policy, based on ideas of economic nationalism, various forms of socialism or, commonly, a mixture of the two.

This is not to argue that Afghanistan was bombed or murderous sanctions imposed on Iraq because they follow protectionist economic policies. It does seem, however, that provided you follow the WTO's rules and edicts NATO will leave you in peace, whatever you are doing to your own citizens or to neighbours.

Notes

1. Introduction to Lori Wallach and Michelle Sforza, *The WTO: Five Years Of Reasons To Resist Corporate Globalization* (Seven Stories Press, 1999)
2. The WTO in Brief, available on the WTO official Website at < http://www.wto.org/english/thewto_e/whatis_e/inbrief_e/inbr00_e.htm >
3. 'What are the Bretton Woods institutions?' at http://www.chebucto.ns.ca/Current/P7/bwi/cccbw.html

5: Globalise This!

> '...this 'anti-authoritarianism' has given the authorities a lot of problems; but the point also needs to be brought out that this structure principally suits the participants – allowing for great momentum of action in what is a diverse movement of groups, organisations and individuals.'
>
> Kevin Doyle [1]

Mass demonstrations, colourful street happenings and violent disturbances greeted the world's trade ministers as they gathered in Seattle for a meeting of the World Trade Organisation Ministerial Conference at the end of November 1999. The demonstrations were on a larger scale and attracted broader support than anything which had occurred previously, but they were not wholly unprecedented. Anti-globalisation had been around as a self-conscious political force since at least 1995, when the routine of gathering outside top-level conferences and summits of political leaders and corporate decision-makers was first established. At Maastricht in 1992, outside the European Community summit which endorsed the thoroughly neoliberal Treaty on European Union, no one demonstrated but the Young European Federalists, a sort of rent-a-mob of well-to-do youth. At Amsterdam five years later tens of thousands gathered and they were far removed from the Chardonnay-quaffing yuppies of YEF. In fact, Amsterdam saw the first high-profile appearance of the anti-globalisation coalition of environmentalists, trade unionists, solidarity organisations, small farmers' groups, trade unions, parties of the left and far left, pacifists, animal rights campaigners, anarchists and many who were active across a range of causes. Amsterdam, also characterised by unusually (for the Dutch) heavy-handed policing and an undercurrent of potential violence, was clearly never going to be a one-off event. To be there was to have a strong feeling that you were witnessing the birth of a new and significant phenomenon, one which would grow into an important political factor as the 21st century arrived.

Amsterdam differed in a number of ways from previous and otherwise comparable mass demonstrations. It was disparate and somewhat unfocussed, with different participating groups making different, sometimes even conflicting, demands. All that brought these people together was their belief that democracy should mean a great deal more than choosing leaders who would best implement decisions taken in faraway, centralised institutions such as the European Commission. For example, when trade unionists demanding a 'social Europe' marched alongside the Dutch Socialist Party, an activist party of the left which views the EU and all its works with disdain, the alliance was less incoherent than it appeared. The feeling was that more Europe or less Europe, it should be 'We the People' (or peoples) that decide. Seattle picked up this ball of democratic indignation and ran with it.

The anti-globalisers were aided by the development, in the meantime, of the kind of technologies which had shown the Dutch authorities that they were dealing with an enemy – which was clearly how they had chosen to view peaceful demonstrators – of increasing sophistication. Once again, globalisation itself equipped those who would halt or transform it with the ability to convey complex information through an instantaneous global communication system. On the day itself mobile phones helped demonstrators to keep one step ahead of the police, while the Internet enabled them to co-ordinate activities in the run-up and compare notes afterwards. In addition, this disparate but gradually coalescing movement was developing disruptive but non-violent forms of protest which were going to require, in turn, new kinds of police response. The battle for the heart and mind of the new century was on.

After Seattle, anti-globalisation demonstrations routinely greeted meetings of the G8, WTO, the IMF, World Bank and other international decision-making bodies. Meetings which in the recent past would be ignored, or perhaps picketed by a handful of people demanding justice for this or that group of people, or protection for one or another endangered species, were now the recurrent targets of what was threatening to become a mass international movement.

The diversity of anti-globalisation activism could have caused problems of disunity and internal strife. Instead, whilst these have not been entirely absent from the movement's experience, diversity has proved, in more than one way, a source of strength. Different groups have been able to learn from each other while, as far as the outside world is concerned, such broad alliances create a powerful impression. This 'new, new left' is activist, highly visible, irreverent, playful and comfortable with diversity, its supporters revelling in the company of people whose background, class, language, nationality, culture and ideas are different to their own. As was evident at Amsterdam, the demand is not so much for a particular programme or approach, but simply for the right to decide. If anti-globalisation lacks a single coherent programme, it is not short of a 'Big Idea' – far-reaching, popular democracy which gives people real control over their lives – or an identifiable enemy, corporate power. Activists differed over priorities, tactics, forms of organisation, but what brought them together was a firm belief that globalisation was the instrument through which corporations consolidated their grip and furthered their ends.

Most of the groups which have built the anti-globalisation movement are small. Memberships are fluid and overlap, and many identifiable 'new, new left' bodies reject traditional forms of organisation and are better perceived as 'rallying points' than as permanent structures. Many of the most militant protesters are focused on what have been defined as 'single issue' campaigns: environmental causes, animal rights, abortion and reproductive rights in general, solidarity movements which concentrate their activities on one country. Yet by looking at, say, the pollution of fresh water courses or the treatment of Amazon-dwellers or Thai garment workers, activists become aware, and make others aware, of the way in which the profit motive, sometimes combined with corrupt or simply unrepresentative government, can override the most basic environmental or humanitarian imperatives; the exploitation and subordination of animals becomes a vivid illustration of the way in which the system instrumentalises everything, for if living, breathing and sometimes appealing animals can be treated as a means to an end, handled as if they were inert things, then why not people? Those who participate in solidarity movements linked to resistance groups in particular countries or regions – Colombia, El Salvador, Nicaragua, Chiapas, East Timor and a host of other countries – do not generally seek to emphasise the uniqueness of a particular people's plight but, on the contrary, its representative nature. This, they are saying, is what the greed of rich nations and corporations is doing to these people and what is being done to them is a typical illustration of how the world works.

Forms of organisation chosen or evolved by the anti-globalisation movements also exhibit certain almost ubiquitous features. Even within the remnants of orthodox pro-Soviet Communism, one finds a rejection of the authoritarianism and centralising tendencies of traditional Leninist party structures, which tend now to be favoured only by small groupings of the far left. To be a member of the Communist Party of Great Britain (or anywhere else) from the 1920s to the 1930s, or a militant of one of the host of Trotskyist or Marxist-Leninist (Maoist) fragments which still exist, it is necessary to accept a certain discipline. This may vary from a simple acceptance of the party or group's tenets and a reasonable level of activity, to a commitment which can come to consume almost every waking minute. Wherever it stands on the continuum, however, it is clearly based on the notion of the party as Leninist vanguard, a body of dedicated individuals whose job is to provide the working class with leadership, and a distinct institution with its own permanent structures, a constitution, a body of ideas and practices distinct from every other group.

Contrast this style with the notorious Black Bloc, less a movement than a tactic. The Black Bloc has no members, no constitution, no permanent structures. To participate, all you have to do is turn up at the right time and place, dress in black, and be prepared to break the law, disobey police instructions and operate in the belief that completely peaceful, orderly protests will invariably be ignored or co-opted. Part of the advantage of the Black Bloc tactic is that it has proved extremely difficult for the authorities, themselves generally structured in military or quasi-military hierarchies, to understand just what it is they are dealing with.

Less hierarchical forms of organisation have undoubtedly been given an additional attraction by the failure of the vertical 'Leninist' party model to bring about lasting and sustained change, at least of a desirable nature, in those societies where it has prevailed. In addition, newly-available technologies have offered the opportunity to experiment, changing the way in which demonstrations are conducted and bringing a radically new style to protest activities in general. The Black Blocs do not, as is well known, shun violence. Yet, unlike for example, certain animal rights groups and activists of far-right racist and anti-abortion campaigns, their violence has been almost entirely directed at property. Even property is rarely attacked indiscriminately, tending to be aimed at banks, other financial institutions, and what are seen as ostentatious displays of wealth, particularly certain marks of car. The great exception, of course, is violence directed against the police themselves. However, anyone who has attended a demonstration where the Black Blocs have been active will affirm that the police are as often the instigators of violence as its victims. In Gothenborg in 2000, the affray appears to have been provoked by a section of demonstrators; in the first major Barcelona demonstration in the same year, police officers were caught on film deliberately starting fights whilst dressed in a way clearly designed to mislead people into thinking they were demonstrators. In Genoa parts of the crowd were attacked by thugs in the uniforms of the Carabinieri, Italy's notorious militarised police force.

Violence against property is reprehensible, but in the case of the Black Blocs and others like them it is far from 'mindless,' the word so often used to describe it in the mainstream press. On the contrary, whether favouring violent or peaceful tactics, anti-globalisation demonstrators have generally pursued aims which are recognisably rooted in the methods favoured by 'non-violent' campaigners such as the Campaign for Nuclear Disarmament (CND), anti-road protesters and, classically, by two of the 20th century's greatest radical leaders, Martin Luther King and Mahatma Gandhi. Developed from these beginnings, 'non-violence' has evolved into a well thought-out set of tactics which often relies on making it difficult for targeted groups and the people defending them simply to get around. Much more than an absence of violence, and in most cases adopted through a belief in its efficacy as a tactic as much as, or rather than, any philosophical commitment to pacifism, 'non-violence' relies on the sheer force of numbers to make it impossible, for example, to hold scheduled meetings. It seeks to make life uncomfortable for pampered politicians and bureaucrats, to disrupt, distract and annoy. Often coupled with playful, colourful demonstrations of street theatre, music and all the juggling, stilt-walking, mask-wearing antics of the early 21st century's broad alternative scene – again, a style which has been greatly influenced by the merging of cultural influences which has been a feature of globalisation – such demonstrations have the advantage of variety and inclusiveness. Even the Black Blocs have co-operated with organisers who have sought to convince them that areas of demonstrations which can be, as far as is possible, guaranteed free of clashes between activists and the police, are necessary so that older people, children and the for whatever reason physically timid can also attend. Targeted cities are often divided into different zones, with one area where authorised demonstrations take place and another where the Black Blocs and others have let it be known that they intend to take on the police or make direct attempts to get closer to the meeting being protested than the authorities have been prepared to allow.

The mainstream media began from a standpoint of hostility to the demonstrations, exaggerating acts of violence and failing to report on the broader picture. Gradually, however, as the demonstrations have become bigger, growing in fact to dwarf anything seen since the 1968 student and worker uprisings or the US Civil Rights and anti-Vietnam War movements, coverage has become generally more balanced and police violence has begun to be reported. Violence in general, from whatever perpetrator, is, however, regarded as much more attractive copy than, for example, an explanation of why many people believe that Third World countries' debts should be cancelled. Moreover, this hunger for sensation is not the only reason why the degree of violence at anti-globalisation demonstrations has been exaggerated. With rare exceptions, TV companies and newspapers are corporate-owned, and therefore cannot always be trusted to report in an objective way on the activities of those who see corporations as the enemy.

The growth of the Internet has offered anti-globalisation groups a way round the growing concentration of ownership in the mainstream media. Webzines such as Indymedia, Labournet, Spectre and Corpwatch carry news on a range of subjects from a left viewpoint. Each Non-Governmental Organisation (NGO), political party and activist group has its own Website, as do many individuals. Information flows further, faster and more freely than ever before and, temporarily at least, this has reduced the imbalance of coverage and opinion.

As well as ideological discussion and information exchange, the Internet has facilitated the physical organisation of demonstrations. Fixing venues, dates and times, sharing tasks and experiences, arranging logistics and support services have all been made less daunting by the existence of this fast, easy to use and relatively cheap system of communication. Anti-globalisation as a consciously international political force could not have come into being without the instantaneous global communication and fast, cheap travel which are themselves a part of the very process which the movement has been created to combat. The Internet also fits with those non-hierarchical and decentralised forms of organisation which have emerged as globalisation's distinctive methodology, facilitating communication and coordination of ideas and plans without the need for expensive or inaccessible resources or a top-heavy decision-making structure.

Since it has become obvious that the great and the good will not be allowed to meet in accessible locations without the accompanying presence of large numbers of demonstrators, international pro-globalisation institutions have taken to planning their get-togethers in mountainous or otherwise remote areas, or hard-to-reach dictatorships such as Oman, where the absence of any freedom of expression makes street demonstrations impossible or at best extremely dangerous. In addition, ordinary inhabitants of major cities have begun to resist being chosen as a venue for G8, IMF, WTO or similar meetings. What once would have been regarded as something of an honour, perhaps, or at least a source of revenue and publicity, is now anticipated with dread. During the mass demonstrations in Barcelona in 2002 and Genoa the previous year, many inhabitants simply decamped, taking their summer holidays or staying with family or friends out of town. Apart from the media-exaggerated but nevertheless real threat of violence, people tend to react with overwhelming indignation to having to endure identity controls, friskings and interrogation simply to be allowed into the street where they live.

Remote and bizarre locations don't necessarily always work, of course. In May, 2000, the annual meeting of the Asian Development Bank (part of the World Bank group) at Chiang Mai, Thailand, was halted by an estimated 5,000 people protesting at what they saw as the Bank's corporate agenda. This was, again, an aspect of globalisation as much as an attempt to halt, reverse or redirect it. Until very recently the ADB might possibly have been picketed by a few activists with leaflets, nervously eyeing a police presence by which they were greatly outnumbered. Thousands turned up instead of a handful because they had seen Seattle and similar events on television and knew via the Internet that the people protesting the WTO had much the same concerns as they did. When, as in Okinawa shortly after this, the relative inaccessibility of a location and the determination of the police make mass protest impossible, it tends to break out elsewhere. In the case of Okinawa, the day before the G8 summit saw protests across Japan.

Anti-Globalisation Groups

The fact that globalisation touches so many aspects of life, that its effects are 'global' in the sense of 'all-embracing' as well as in the geographic sense, is what has provoked resistance from such a wide range of groups. A few of these are worth examining more closely.

World Social Forum

Increasingly seen as a co-ordinating body seeking to bring together reformist, radical and revolutionary voices from every country, the World Social Forum was only formally established in 2001, when it held its first meeting in Porto Alegre, Brazil. An initiative of the powerful left-wing opposition Brazilian Workers' Party – which governs the city and the state where it is located, Rio Grande de Sul – and a range of NGOs and movements for change, the WSF gathered in Porto Alegre for a second time just over a year later. It is now firmly established as an international body which brings together militants, political parties, parliamentarians, NGOs… anyone, in fact, seeking to resist globalisation, or to control it for progressive ends, whether through reform, revolution or some radical course between the two. Its global gatherings are timed to coincide with the World Economic Forum (WEF), a body which enables business people and mainstream political leaders to gather behind closed doors to discuss a range of topics of mutual interest.

The WEF, also known as 'Davos' after the small Swiss town where until recently it gathered, is seen by the people behind the WSF as undemocratic and secretive, a means whereby big corporations and their friends in government can work out a corporate-friendly agenda and plan how to execute it. The rise of the anti-globalisation movement and the determination of some activists to protest as near as possible to WEF's cosy private chats created a security problem of such dimensions that the Swiss government asked the Forum to find somewhere else to meet. The WSF is, in contrast, open, with a structure modelled on ideas of participatory democracy, the rights of minorities, and a thoroughgoing egalitarianism. So far it has generated no security problems to speak of.

The open structure of the Forum, with its inclusive slogan 'Another World Is Possible,' gives it an impressively representative face far removed from the corporate clones of Davos. It does, however, leave it somewhat vulnerable to mainstream politicians seeking to convince participants that they too are opposed to the 'excesses' of globalisation, or that it isn't really globalisation which is the enemy at all. Even free market enthusiasts such as Belgian Prime Minister Guy Verhofstadt have expressed an interest in the Forum. More credibly, the authoritative left-wing French monthly *Le Monde Diplomatique* has been one of the prime movers behind the initiative, while funds have come from bodies as respectable as the Dutch Organisation for International Development Cooperation, Novib.

The Forum's two gatherings have been held in each case over several days, with workshops on the various aspects of globalisation. The 2002 Forum, for instance, organised its sessions around four themes: the production and distribution of wealth; access to wealth and sustainable development; civil society and the public arena; and political power and ethics. Tens of thousands of participants took part in a total of 5,000 workshops, while demonstrations and rallies tried to make as many people as possible aware of the WSF and its aims.

ATTAC

ATTAC began life as, and ostensibly remains, a movement with a single goal, the introduction of a small levy on cross-border capital transactions along the lines suggested by Nobel economics laureate James Tobin. The Tobin Tax remains at the centre of ATTAC's work, but since the movement's foundation in 1999 it has broadened to become one of the principle vehicles of anti-globalisation. In addition, the Tobin Tax envisaged by the radical left thinkers and activists of ATTAC is rather different to that proposed by James Tobin, whose aim was certainly not to question the overall desirability of capitalism or the free market. On the contrary, Tobin was looking for a way of preventing the kind of stock market volatility which more than anything gives the impression that this same system is uncontrollable and ought to be replaced, or at least severely modified. Tobin's proposal was for a tax of between 0.1% and 0.25%, which he believed would raise enough cash to enable governments to mitigate the effects of speculation, whilst being insufficient to deter investment.

Despite the Nobel Prize, Tobin's idea was pushed into the margins of mainstream economics by the liberalising, deregulating frenzy of the 1980s. Capital must be free to wonder where it would, and governments seeking to impose a tax, however modest, on cross-border transactions would be likely to find themselves penalised by investors. Only concerted international action could avoid this, and with the world's biggest economies – the US, Japan, Germany and Britain amongst them – in the hands of governments of the neoliberal right, this was an unlikely prospect. For all their talk of free trade, the EU, US, Japan and others were, and remain, prepared to slap tariffs on imported goods whenever it suits them, and whilst lecturing the Third World about the virtues of free trade, to discriminate against goods from developing countries. Free movement of capital had, however, acquired an almost religious status which was more than mere lip-service.

During the 1990s, with the resurgence of the centre-left in Europe and North America, discussion of speculation and its attendant problems ceased to be confined to the political margins. In December, 1997, Ignacio Ramonet, editor of *Le Monde Diplomatique*, wrote an opinion piece which can be seen as the beginning of ATTAC, its conception if not its birth. Ramonet pointed out that a tax of only 0.1% on exchange transactions would produce a return of $228 billion dollars annually. But Ramonet also had ideas about how the money could be spent. 1.7 billion people in the world were living below the UN's somewhat arbitrary 'absolute poverty' level of a dollar a day, and the ethical way to use the resources amassed through a tax on capital movements which affected these people's interests but over which they had no control, was in improving their lot. The Association for a Tobin Tax in Aid of Citizens (ATTAC) was founded six months later, bringing together NGOs, progressive publications, trade unions and individuals, many of them well known.

It is easy to see how this apparently single-issue pressure group has become something more, something far broader. The Tobin Tax has attracted support from some people who are relatively happy with globalisation, social democratic politicians who, like UK Development Minister Clare Short, argue that globalisation is inevitable but can be tamed and made to work for the greater good. One reason for that is its apparent reasonableness. ATTAC is not demanding a return to the system of exchange controls which operated in most of the world before the Thatcher-Reagan transformation of the global economy in the 1980s. Tariffs in general can have two functions: to raise revenue, or to exclude. Set too high a tax on inward investment or export of capital and you won't raise a penny, because such movements will cease. The level of the Tobin Tax was clearly chosen to ensure that its actual effects on capital movements would be negligible.

Yet no one in power would take it seriously. What seemed to many a rather mild proposal was rejected out of hand. This led some who had been attracted to it to question the prevailing order. Why could such a tiny fraction of such vast wealth not be diverted to help pull the desperately poor out of their predicament and into the world? Surely, even TNCs might find some merit in a measure which could enable millions to join the great consumer game?

Because of this the Tobin Tax idea not only attracted radicals, it created them. The Tobin Tax became a rallying point for a resurgent internationalism, one of the cornerstones of the anti-globalisation phenomenon. At ATTAC's founding event in June 1998, around eighty countries and a range of organisations were represented, described by one speaker as 'an international archipelago of human struggle.'

ATTAC's success can be measured in the number of articles which now appear in newspapers such as the *Financial Times* and *Wall Street Journal* dismissing Tobin's idea. Three years ago they were ignoring it.

Via Campesina

Founded in 1992, Via Campesina differs from ATTAC and the WSF in a number of ways. Firstly, it seeks to bring together a particular group of people identifiable by their means of livelihood rather than through a common set of beliefs. Though its members tend to be left-leaning and anti-authoritarian, membership is open to all farmers internationally who do not form part of the large-scale agribusiness nexus that increasingly dominates world food production and distribution. In addition, it welcomes landless agricultural labourers and other rural inhabitants, and lays great emphasis on the rights of indigenous peoples and, in particular, of the women who form the backbone of the world's farm labour force. Via Campesina now claims members in Asia, Africa, America and Europe, and has succeeded in identifying live issues capable of uniting farmers across barriers of culture and experience.

Via Campesina's principal objective is to develop solidarity between different small farmers' organisations in pursuit of what it defines as just and equitable economic and social relations, environmental values including land conservation, sustainable farming methods and 'food sovereignty,' defined as the ability of peoples to decide their own forms of government and to take other fundamental decisions in the knowledge that no outside force can menace them by cutting off their access to food. If this seems melodramatic, it should be understood that what concerns Via Campesina most is not the possibility of Iraqi-style sanctions or an embargo such as that which Cuba has had to endure for over forty years. Though these two cases demonstrate that such threats exist, Via Campesina sees more mundane threats to food sovereignty in the introduction, for example, of what it sees as 'inappropriate technologies,' such as genetic modification or the growing of crops that require expensive and possibly dangerous pesticides or chemical fertilisers. Such techniques require repeated and sustained inputs from corporate sources, and for farmers in the South in particular this means from sources whose decision-makers live far, far away – and not only in the strictly literal, geographic sense.

Via Campesina can sometimes be seen on anti-globalisation demonstrations, but it also works more conventionally, by lobbying and attempting to persuade and put pressure on elected politicians and other decision-makers. In doing so it has shown itself highly skilled in the use of modern electronic media, adaptable in the way it presents its arguments, willing to use both parliamentary and extra-parliamentary means to achieve its end and thus, as with its decentralised structure, in many ways typical of the broad movement of which it forms a part.

Finally, perhaps the feature of Via Campesina which makes it representative of the anti-globalisation style is the way in which it has developed what were 'one-way' solidarity movements into a two-way form of cooperation. The traditional solidarity movement consists of sympathetic people in the prosperous countries of the North using the resources that such prosperity brings, as well as the relatively large space for freedom of expression and organisation enjoyed in most western democracies, to draw attention to the plight of poor people in the Third World. Via Campesina goes beyond this, organising around the principle that, even if most small farmers in Europe or North America are materially far better off than their confreres in the South, their livelihoods and ways of life are menaced by precisely the same processes. Experience has shown that such movements, based on cooperation around common goals rather than one group's sympathy with the situation of another, are more durable.

Indymedia

As with so many arms of the anti-globalisation movement, Indymedia is both a product of globalisation and a response to it. As the mainstream media become more concentrated in corporate hands, representing, as with the parliamentary political spectrum, an ever-narrower range of views, more and more people are taking advantage of the Internet and related information technologies to express different points of view, publicise and organise resistance, and promote discussion.

Indymedia is written by its readers. In theory, there is no reason why it should not carry comment favouring the kind of policies to which the anti-globalisation movement is opposed, and such material does indeed sometimes appear. In practice, however, debate tends to assume a standpoint within a certain radical range. There is a good reason for this. Neoliberal views already dominate the print and broadcast media and their exponents do not need Indymedia. Opponents of the corporate domination of the mainstream argue that it serves to exclude the majority of people's voices. There is, however, a ready response: the fact is, this argument goes, that most people do not share the radical views of Indymedia 'types' and therefore such information sources are no more representative than are the mass circulation newspapers and popular broadcast media. After all, these are popular because people buy them, read them, watch them. There are, in turn, many answers to this, referring to broader relations of power, control of education

71

systems, and so on. However, the real answer is far simpler: no one is excluded from the mainstream media if they wish to express their agreement with prevailing ideas, or to flatter the powerful. Indymedia deals as much in excluded ideas as in excluded voices.

In most parts of the world, people have learnt to exploit new, affordable technologies to create alternative media. Websites that are updated weekly, daily or several times a day carry news, commentary and announcements of demonstrations, meetings and other events. Prominent examples include the UK weekly *Schnews*, the 'World Socialist Website,' the Belgian-based English language weekly *Spectre*, and the American *Corpwatch*. However, to list them all would fill another book. In addition, community and unlicensed 'pirate' radio stations reach people who cannot afford Internet access, videos record events ignored or, in the independent media view, distorted by the mainstream. In the US, in addition, the video- or audio-recording of speeches by major left figures such as Noam Chomsky, Ralph Nader or Barbara Ehrenreich has become commonplace, with tapes then being made available at cost price to activists across the country and beyond. Transcripts are routinely made of radio interviews and then distributed through the Internet. Listservers which collect material from both mainstream and alternative sources – such as Florida Left List, Labor Notes and a huge number of 'single issue campaign' oriented briefings – can be sent to hundreds, thousands, or potentially even millions of people at the click of a mouse.

Again, Seattle proved a step forward for what has been called 'DIY media.' The Seattle Independent Media Center (IMC) experimented with an open publishing system which allowed anyone with Internet access to upload photographs, audio and video files directly to the its Website, enabling them to communicate both with each other and with the wider world beyond the demonstrations. The model was a great success, receiving 1.5 million hits in the few days around the actions, many from mainstream journalists who, like Bob Dylan's famous reporter 'Mr Jones,' knew something was happening but not what on earth it was.

Using the same system to cover big gatherings in the UK and US – with some refinements, such as the placing of 'Public Access Terminals' in the thick of the action, so that people could report their experiences while, so to speak, they were still having them – activists who had begun with the aim of balancing largely hostile or uncomprehending mainstream reports of particular events found that they had planted the seeds of something more permanent. Indymedia was born. Typical of the anti-globalisation movement which had given it life, the bouncing baby was a decentralised collection of loosely affiliated groups sharing ideas, software and other technology, techniques and a commitment to reporting things as they saw them.

By 2002, IMCs had been created in most major US cities as well as in Belgium, the UK, Italy and France, and a growing number of other countries. Print and broadcast media may be in the hands of the globalisers, but the Internet, at least, remains an open forum through which ideas can be discussed, experiences shared and resistance organised. With its anarchic feel, relatively low costs, varying reliability, inherently decentralised structure and ability to connect two or two million people instantly across the globe, the Internet is not only anti-globalisation's principal tool, it also serves as a fitting symbol for the movement as a whole.

Note

1. In a review of Kevin Danaher and Roger Burback, *Globalise This! - The Battle Against The WTO And Corporate Rule* (Common Courage Press). The review appeared in *Red And Black Revolution* 5 and is online at < http://flag.blackened.net/revolt/rbr/rbr5/globalise.html >

6: Battlefields

'The world has changed since the Bretton Woods agreement: The present international, economic, financial and political architecture of the world, (including the World Bank, the IMF and other institutions), was largely set up in the 1940s, following the Bretton Woods Conference in 1944. The bulk of Asia and Africa was still under imperialist dominance then; tolerance of insecurity and poverty was much greater; the idea of human rights was still very weak; the power of NGOs had not yet emerged; the environment was not seen as particularly important; and democracy was definitely not seen as a global entitlement.'

Amartya Sen [1]

Globalisation touches not only almost every corner of the world, but every issue too. To make sense of it, it is possible to focus on certain key questions around which the globalisation debate revolves. The first, and most urgent of these, is debt.

Debt

Most 'developing' countries have very large debts. Debt has, in reality halted development in its tracks, yet the amount of money owed by poor countries continues to increase. Servicing debt, through attempts at repayment or simply trying to keep up with accumulating interest, prevents countries from addressing immediate problems such as malnutrition or inadequate sanitation. It also means that they cannot find the money to make the infrastructural investments needed to raise living standards, in education, healthcare, transport systems, scientific research or simply improving the capacity of the state or non-state institutions to deliver improved services or make ambitions into reality. Sub-Saharan Africa alone pays $10 billion every year in debt service, about four times as much money as goes on healthcare and education. [2]

Although there is a great deal of sympathy in the mainstream media and amongst western politicians for the plight of countries caught in the debt trap, blame tends to be directed at the victims, or at least at what is seen as a home-grown corrupt elite. Many post-colonial countries have had to suffer rule by elites who, seizing the state, abandon all but the shakiest pretence of using it for any purpose other than to subjugate the rest of the population and line their own pockets. This does not, however, excuse the western banks, governments and international financial institutions who encouraged such behaviour by not making, or enforcing, any real standards, and by pushing governments, in response to the irresolvable debt crises provoked in part by such irresponsible lending, into adopting monetarist policies which bear heavily upon those least able to shoulder the burden.

The group of countries which have suffered most from this process includes those oil exporters who, up until the 1970s, seemed most likely to make the leap from Third to First World. Western industrialised nations, however, had little interest in encouraging further industrialisation or other forms of economic diversification, which they saw as the deliberate creation of competitors. Instead, countries with surplus capital were encouraged to export it, lodging it in western banks which lent it to other, poorer developing countries. Much of this money went on misguided, environmentally disastrous and socially insensitive mega-projects, including dams. Pleas that real development would come from tackling widespread, small-scale problems, were ignored or rejected in favour of ill-thought out energy projects, roads which went nowhere, and technologies which could be sustained only with continual input from the TNCs which developed and manufactured them. Obvious priorities, such as the delivery of clean drinking water to everyone, investment in the most productive labour (in other words, in women and girls), and the addressing of natural hazards (flooding, earthquakes, hurricanes, volcanoes and so on) with a view to reducing loss of life and damage to property, were shunned in favour of projects where the biggest beneficiaries were shareholders of the TNCs involved. At the same time, rising world interest rates, a global recession and low commodity prices pushed effective debt ever upwards. The obligation to repay in tradable 'hard' currency, the tendency of Third World countries' currencies to decline in value (making external debt effectively more expensive), and a secular downward trend in the prices of the kind of primary commodities on which many have been forced to rely have all contributed to untenable levels of indebtedness.

Initiatives to deal with the debt crisis might be divided into three groups. Enthusiasts for globalisation portray it as the way out of debt, and SAPs as the 'pain' without which 'gain' is proverbially impossible. Reformers call for debt relief for the poorest, the so-called LDCs, the Least Developed Countries. Certain NGOs and the United Nations' child poverty arm UNICEF have proposed various debt relief programmes, notably UNICEF's Debt for Child Relief, an agreement with certain banks whereby they would receive tax deductions for transferring the debts due to them to UNICEF. UNICEF then collects the debt repayments in local currency and spends it on programmes to help children inside the country. Anti-globalisers, however, question the legitimacy of debts which result in more wealth flowing from poor to rich countries than vice versa, debt servicing adding up to more than the combined value of inward investment, aid and trade. In general they call, through groups such as Jubilee 2000 or the more radical Campaign for the Abolition of Third World Debt (known as CADTM, its French acronym), for a complete cancellation of poor countries' debts. Debts, they argue, were generally contracted by undemocratic, authoritarian regimes which used the money to buy arms to continue repressing their people, or simply salted it away in Swiss bank accounts, often with the connivance of western governments. Most countries in this plight, moreover, have already repaid far more than they ever borrowed. By 1994, indebted developing countries were annually paying out over $100 billion more than they received. [3]

Food

The vital issue of the control of the food supply has, as much as debt, dominated the globalisation debate. Ideally, anti-globalisers such as Via Campesina would like to see farmers able to take decisions about what to grow and how to grow it, free from interference from powerful TNCs. The preconditions for such autonomy can, in this view, be provided only if the land is owned and controlled by the people who work it, and if the technologies which they employ are appropriate. In the case of poor farmers in poor countries, appropriate technology means something which may have been developed through traditional knowledge, or by the most advanced research techniques available to 21st-century science or, as is so often the case, by a marriage of the two. The crucial question is not where the technology comes from but to what extent it is manageable by the women and men who work the land, to what extent it needs further inputs from outside and, if it does need such inputs, who is controlling their availability. An ideal technology would therefore be, say, a machine which increases productivity and which can be repaired using easily understood techniques and readily-available materials, or a method of organisation which raises yields without relying on something which must be repeatedly purchased from outside.

By the same token, the worst kinds of technology are those which must be repeatedly supplied by western TNCs, which cannot be controlled by people lacking the highly specialised education and training typical of western scientists, engineers or technicians, and which carry with them at least the possibility of new, unpredictable environmental hazards. Which explains why, aside from the question of land reform, the issue of genetically modified crops has come to acquire such significance.

Whatever the rights and wrongs of the debate about GMOs as it impinges on questions of human, animal or plant health or on broader environmental questions, one thing is certain: their cultivation will reinforce the dependence of farmers on TNCs. Only the people who developed this technology can control it. Gene splicing is not something the average Indonesian smallholder is able to do in her own kitchen. In the anti-globalisers' view, the patenting of genetically engineered organisms or the foodstuffs and other products based on them threatens to consign farming as it has been practised for perhaps 15,000 years to the dustbin of history. Farmers who have always reused seeds from the previous crop, and who have extensive knowledge of the ways in which yields can be maximised, inputs reduced and labour kept to a minimum, will instead be forced to buy GM seeds and associated chemicals from one of a small number of TNCs. At the same time, the patenting of transgenic plants and even animals will reinforce this dependence, forcing farmers to lease their plants and livestock from biotech conglomerates, paying royalties on seeds and other necessities. The likely result is that ever more small farmers will be driven off the land.

Ownership and control of the land is the other great food-related issue of the globalisation era. If GM technology enables TNCs to control what is grown and how, the concentration of land ownership on which the undemocratic structures of most developing countries have long rested allows powerful elites to determine where and how. By attaching conditions to loans or contracts, farmers who fear for their own or their families' health are forced to use pesticides which they suspect, or know, to be inimical to health. Deception and bullying force farmers, who would prefer to stick to what they know and can control, to switch to GM crops through the same means or, more simply, by deception or terror or both.

Globalisers reply that GM has the potential to increase outputs and thus 'feed the world.' This ignores the fact that, for the time being at least, there is easily enough food to go round, the problem being rather that it is unevenly distributed. People go hungry because they are too poor to buy food, and not, save in short-lived crises often precipitated by war or natural disaster, because there isn't any food to be had. Yet, even if it is true that GM could increase yields and that we may well soon reach a point where the absolute number of calories available for consumption is simply not enough to go round, this does not mean that biotechnology offers the only, or the best solution. Huge amounts of land are wasted through the growing of unnecessary crops using unsustainable techniques. Countries such as Kenya, where malnutrition is common, now use large amounts of land and water to grow flowers for Europeans who can't get through winter without them. Valentine's Day, coming in the depths of the northern winter, takes bread from the mouths of African children with every lovelorn bunch of blooms.

Biotechnology has led to the neglect of other possible solutions to hunger and the research needed to develop them. The Green Revolution of the 1960s certainly reduced the immediate problem of hunger, but longer-term nutritional and environmental problems have since appeared which can be directly traced to its innovations. Ironically, the vitamin deficiency which results in the form of blindness for which the genetically engineered crop known as Golden Rice would offer a solution was brought about by the labelling of numerous useful plants as weeds. These had been gathered near fields or even growing amongst planted crops, but with the Green Revolution they were eliminated.

In the same way, even if GM increases yields, it will almost certainly bring unpredicted problems in its wake. These will in turn require another 'technological fix.' At every step the poor farmer, if she manages to hang on to her land, becomes more dependent, less able to take the decisions experience tells her are the correct ones – not correct from the point of view of TNC shareholders, perhaps, but correct from the point of view of her family, of the children who are the only real guarantee that she will have any kind of future at all.

Work

During the 20th century the provision of work, or at least the creation of conditions favourable to a high level of employment, was seen as being amongst the major tasks of government. Recently, this has begun to change. Whilst much lip-service continues to be paid to the role of political factors in employment creation, this has now come to mean something quite different to the interventionist strategies which prevailed for decades until the emergence of the Thatcher-Reagan ideological axis in the 1980s. Governments have, in fact, systematically deprived themselves of a range of instruments traditionally used to combat unemployment and to ensure that available labour does not go unused by: privatising publicly owned services, industries and property; in the case of most EU countries, surrendering control of interest and exchange rates to the European Central Bank, an institution constitutionally obliged to make a low rate of inflation its absolute, unchanging priority; and signing up to international agreements – the Treaty of Rome, the WTO, NAFTA and others – which make state aids in most cases illegal. In the name of preventing unfair competition, most interventionist strategies have been declared out of bounds or made extremely difficult.

The reasoning behind this is simple. Jobs are created in dynamic economies. Subsidies prop up ailing industries and create long-term problems, even if they temporarily alleviate unemployment. If a country subsidises an inefficient industry, or protects it behind tariff barriers, it prevents efficient industries elsewhere from flourishing and prevents capital from being invested in more productive sectors. The wealth of nations is increased, as Adam Smith argued, when everyone does what they're best at. And everyone does what they're best at when the free market and free trade are allowed to prevail.

This means that employment can be generated only on the back of economic growth. In turn, economic growth can only happen when the economy is allowed to operate efficiently, when markets are deregulated and enterprise encouraged. If employers have to pay too much in social insurance contributions, or if they are overly burdened by the 'red tape' of unnecessary and expensive legal requirements, they will be unable to operate efficiently and generate jobs. In particular, any social payments which increase with the number of employees a firm has represent a 'tax on jobs.'

Proponents of the free market argue that employment is the only sustainable route out of poverty both for individuals and countries. The market will always deliver the wages and conditions which are affordable, and any attempt to interfere with this process will do more harm than good. In this view transnational corporate activity provides the means to such development. If local firms are driven out of business this is only because they are inefficient. The benefits they may bring are illusory, because they prevent the emergence of more dynamic indigenous enterprise and the abandonment of practices which hold back development and which pander to vested interests at the expense of everyone else. TNCs provide jobs directly, of course, but they also do so indirectly through the taxes they pay, technology transfer, earning foreign currency and creating a need for infrastructure which everyone can then use.

Anti-corporate activists point out that instances of TNC interference in the sovereign affairs of nations poor and rich have invariably been directed at curtailing or modifying the kind of policies which aim to narrow disparities in wealth, improve labour conditions and generally better the lot of working men and women and their families. TNCs use their influence to encourage what has been called a 'race to the bottom' or a game of 'beggar my neighbour,' in which countries compete to attract business by offering the cheapest labour and the least 'red tape.'

Transnational corporations are estimated to provide, through direct employment, only 2% to 3% of the world's jobs, though if all of the economic activity they generate is taken into account, the figure is perhaps twice this. That 2-3% represents around 73 million jobs, but only twelve million of these are in developing countries. This figure also fails to take into account the possibility that some livelihoods may be destroyed by TNC activities where, for example, local businesses are unable to compete and go to the wall, or where farmers are displaced to make way for commercial operations.

TNCs are, however, key employers in a number of countries and in some industrial sectors. The seemingly low figure quoted above is distorted by the inclusion of agricultural sectors, where much activity remains outside corporate hands, though this grows less each year. Take away farming and it rises to 20%. In other words, in industry, commerce and non-farm services one in five of the world's wage workers gets his or her pay cheque from a transnational corporate employer.

Far from showing a steady tendency to increase, the numbers employed by TNCs are actually falling as a result of both technologies which increase productivity and thus decrease the need for labour, and the spread of liberalising, deregulating political ideologies designed, in part, to make labour easier to shed.

Taking everything into consideration, it may be that TNCs account for between 5% and 6% of the world's jobs. On the other hand, they control as much as a third of total global productive capacity. The imbalance between the two figures demonstrates that corporate claims to bring employment and prosperity are self-serving and inaccurate. [4]

And then, of course, there are jobs and there are jobs. Counting the number of jobs created by a TNC or other body disguises the obvious fact that the figure will include both those who do fulfilling work for good pay in clean, warm offices and enjoy a package of benefits such as healthcare, paid holidays, pension rights and those who must work for barely a living wage in dangerous or otherwise unpleasant conditions, and for whom getting sick means not a few days off at the expense of employer or state, but a personal financial catastrophe. On this count, TNCs, despite severe criticism of their employment practices from solidarity movements targeting particular corporations or sectors, seem to do better. North and South, TNCs on average provide higher wages, safer working conditions and more attractive benefit packages than do local firms. So why does an organisation such as the (mainly European) Clean Clothes Campaign, which tries to improve the lot of Third World garment workers, or the US-based Students Against Sweatshops, single TNCs out for criticism?

Firstly, the raw figures, which seem to reflect well on corporate employers, tell only part of the story. TNCs often provide higher wages in developed countries simply because they have mainly concentrated their activities on higher-skill sectors where you would expect to find unionised workforces whose training makes them difficult to replace. In developing countries, TNCs can quickly outstrip local productivity levels through their access to technology, novel forms of organisation in the workplace and old-fashioned economies of scale.

The catch is that, though it is indisputable that TNCs in general offer better pay, if levels of remuneration are compared to productivity, the picture starts to look rather different. Though workers may be taking home a fatter pay packet than those doled out by local firms, they will for the most part be receiving a lower share of their employers' profits. This may not seem of any great importance to the worker who can now afford a new dress, medicine for a sick parent or child, or an ice-cold beer at the end of a hot shift, but in the long term it is crucial to an economy's development. The employee might not grudge the boss or shareholder an even greater leap of wealth if he or she is earning more than ever before. But while income from wages mainly remains in the country, TNC profits for the most part don't. In addition, if TNCs are paying the going rate to attract highly skilled and managerial staff who could emigrate with relative ease to the rich North, then paying wages which represent a low share of the corporation's overall income can only contribute to widening disparities of wealth and power, and thus to instability, dissatisfaction and social polarisation.

TNCs also use their political muscle to establish arrangements which may mean that they are not subject to the same rules as local employers. Most will happily use repressive regimes to deny their employees the right to organise and to intimidate those who attempt to defy this. Such rules as do exist are evaded through a variety of means including contracting out parts of the production process, failing to cooperate with compliance regimes and straightforward bribery. In many developing countries Export

Processing Zones (EPZs) have been established, areas where normal labour standards do not apply and TNCs and others can pay below the minimum wage and avoid irksome sections of the labour code. Even outside these zones, however, a low rate of unionisation, a lack of political will or a failure to find the resources or build the capacity needed to maintain effective inspectorates make flouting the law easy.

There are some exceptions. Globalisation has not only brought the downside of industrialisation in a free market system to numerous developing countries, it has also spread ideas and techniques for organisation inside the workplace and beyond. When the car industry was first established in Brazil in the 1970s, for instance, the United Auto Workers of America ensured that the people hired to work in it were familiar with methods of organisation and collective bargaining which had helped to lift their own members out of poverty within living memory. There were retired American car workers who could remember their own successful attempts, in the mid-1930s, to unionise and the huge jump in living standards and quality of working conditions that that had brought. Brazilian workers could learn how to deal with Ford Motor Company and others from people who had been doing just that for four decades or more. This interesting example of 'know-how transfer' led to Brazil's first system of employee representation and to the creation of a core of confident, relatively prosperous workers which has transformed the country's political geography. From a military dictatorship, Brazil has evolved some way towards becoming a multi-party democracy in which a progressive working-class party is able to play a full and open role.

Some TNCs have a reputation for treating their employees with a reasonable amount of respect and for paying higher wages than they could hope to earn doing anything else, as well as offering some job security and benefits. Others have loudly trumpeted voluntary Codes of Conduct, but evidence, as well as common sense, indicates that these are rarely enforced or effective. The Brazilian example is the most telling. What it shows is that if TNCs were really serious about treating their employees in developing countries fairly they would use their influence to insist on their right to organise. They would follow the example of Ford, which is said to have refused cooperation with the then-military regime's policy of outlawing independent unionism and persecuting those who tried to defy or change this situation. Ford clearly looked at the alternatives and decided that a stable system of labour relations based on an open bargaining process was preferable to the permanent instability that is life under repressive, corrupt rulers.

If efficiency were the only way to improve competitiveness, then deregulation might be an effective tool. Unfortunately, companies and states can also compete with each other to see who can most cut wages and benefits, get away with the lowest social spending or inflict the worst working conditions. Moreover, it might reasonably be asked whether making it easier to sack people, for which 'deregulation of the labour market' is largely a euphemism, is really the best way to create employment. Perhaps it is; perhaps it is true that thousands of employers are dissuaded from hiring millions of workers by the knowledge that, if they turn out to be unsatisfactory, or surplus to requirements, they cannot be sacked at will. Yet if so, the unemployed themselves must be remarkably short-sighted. In two centuries of industrialisation, demonstrations by people demanding work have not given rise to a single banner calling for deregulation or liberalisation nor has a single slogan been chanted in support of the sort of policies neoliberals claim would solve the problem. Perhaps the supporters of deregulation have taken the demand for jobs too literally, and that what people actually want are decent jobs which allow them to earn a living doing something of which they can be proud in reasonably safe conditions and in the employment of people who respect their dignity. Experience would indicate that whilst making it cheap to hire workers may create jobs, the likely outcome is that unemployed workers become precariously employed workers. Whether this can be seen as an improvement is largely a matter of political opinion and, for the individuals involved, personal temperament.

War

After the first explosion of war in the Arabian Gulf, when Iraq invaded Kuwait, then-President George Bush (the elder) declared that victory over the Iraqi 'Rogue State' was the first step in the creation of a New World Order of peace and prosperity. Ten years and several wars later, it appears that the President may have been over-optimistic.

The Middle East is torn by seemingly permanent strife. While Israel breaks UN resolutions with impunity, Saddam Hussein continues in power and respect for human rights or any form of democracy is almost absent across the entire region. In Yugoslavia, Milosevic has been removed and an uneasy peace has settled but on the ruined remains of what until recently was a peaceful, stable nation.

We are told that September 11th changed everything but this is unlikely to be understood in those many parts of the world which have witnessed, in the last decade, the might of America's armed forces. If globalisation were to mean anything positive in this respect, it would surely be that decisions of a military or quasi-military nature, from sanctions to all-out war, would no longer be taken unilaterally. Instead, there would be a clear process of co-operation capable of bringing to the highest level of international relations the values of democracy and respect – human rights that are claimed as the moral impulse which makes even violent acts against civilians in some cases acceptable.

The era of globalisation has seen a bipolar world, whose fragile peace was maintained by the mutual fear of the horrors of nuclear war, replaced by a world in which there is only one superpower. The United States have shown that they are quite prepared to act unilaterally, even in open defiance of their allies. When Russia and China vetoed a US proposal to allow the bombing and invasion of Yugoslavia, the United States persuaded NATO to sanction the action, a decision which clearly breached their own Charter. Undoubtedly, if NATO had refused this, the US would have attacked Yugoslavia on their own.

This seems less a New World Order than a return to the law of the jungle, which the United Nations was established to try to prevent. There were terrible crimes committed in Kosovo and earlier in other parts of former Yugoslavia, though not all of them were by Serbs. Saddam Hussein is a vicious dictator. Many people felt extremely frustrated by having to watch terrible atrocities being committed in Bosnia, then Kosovo, just as they were pleased that a country with a large army (Iraq) could not invade a small, defenceless neighbour (Kuwait) and simply get away with it. They were horrified by September 11th and wanted to see those responsible caught and punished. If globalisation meant that one powerful country was willing to risk its soldiers' lives and to spend billions of dollars in bringing such people to heel, then this was surely an aspect of the process which we can welcome and celebrate. No longer would we be forced to stare bewildered and helpless as barbarous acts filled out television screens. No longer would we have to cry, in despair, 'Why doesn't somebody do something?'

Or would we? In the last decade, the United States have launched three major military actions, against the Serbian rump of Yugoslavia, against Iraq and against Afghanistan. In each case the governments of these countries were in the hands of people who had shown themselves willing to do some very unpleasant things to get their way. Yet India, Israel, Indonesia, the Soviet Union, post-Soviet Russia, Turkey and others have also invaded neighbours and/or inflicted terrible suffering on large sections of their own populations – and with complete impunity. Powerful countries escape the wrath of the US because the likely consequences of military conflict are unthinkable. Weaker ones do so if they are loyal NATO members or otherwise do America's bidding. Even leaving aside the fact that the US has, time and again, shown itself willing to support dictators who suit their interests, or remove democratically elected governments which displease it, this does not seem much of a basis for a New World Order of ethical foreign policies and equitable international relations.

If the US and its immediate allies – which usually means only the UK – are unable to bend international law to their will, they simply ignore it, or pretend that it says something that it does not. The US has, for example, repeatedly claimed that its attacks on Afghanistan are sanctioned by the right to self-defence, which is indeed enshrined in the UN Charter. This is false, however, as the wording of the relevant article clearly applies only to a country which is under attack and only during such an attack.

A cornerstone of international law is the Helsinki Final Act, unanimously agreed in 1975 by thirty-five European and North American countries. This included a pledge that signatories would never breach another state's borders, or threaten such action. Its principal purpose was to guarantee national borders in Europe which had been established or confirmed after World War Two. It died with Yugoslavia.

Perhaps, it might be argued, this is the New World Order, where dry old treaties are superseded by moral force, where outraged populations push governments into taking action, including military action, to stop terrible abuses, to round up terrorists, to make the world a safer place. Aside from the fact, which I have tried to illustrate above, that this principle, if it is in play at all, is applied very selectively and only against those who do not count themselves allies of the US, this idea, of a sort of ad hoc militarised humanitarianism, is dangerously easy to manipulate to serve whatever happens to be the prevailing interest of a particular day.

Most of us who are privileged to do so value living in relatively stable, law-abiding societies and so respond positively when our political leaders speak of the importance of 'stability' and the 'rule of law.' We should remember, however, that one person's stability can be another's deadening lack of opportunity, and that laws are made by people, people who sometimes have self-serving ends.

Transnational Corporations, which, as we have seen, are central to the process of globalisation, also value stability and the rule of law. Globalisation can, of course, itself be a destabilising factor. By widening the gap in wealth both within and between individual countries it has provoked social unrest, large-scale migration, the transformation of the economic base of whole societies, the destruction of some industries and the migration of others, all factors which contribute to instability. In response to such instability, armed conflicts have emerged. These are rarely between nations, much more often within them. A major factor in creating the conditions for the Yugoslav wars of the 1990s, for example, was the international financial institutions' pressure on Yugoslavia's government to privatise and deregulate through a 'short sharp shock' which threw hundreds of thousands out of work. Attempts to restrict the migration of people from poorer to richer countries, or away from war and repression to more open and peaceful societies, are threatening to escalate into a kind of war in themselves. Police and border forces are becoming more militarised and less respectful of human rights and, indeed, their own laws. The post-September 11 'War on Terrorism' has taken the form of a global upsurge in the adoption and implementation of repressive laws and practices, providing the pretext for the systematic weakening, removal or flouting of civil rights, including in countries with reputations for openness and tolerance. Again, US power has been boosted, with any attempt by other countries to question repressive practices being greeted with righteous indignation and, often, the most breathtaking arrogance. The United States is the one country which has stated that it does not regard the actions of its citizens to be bound by decisions of the newly-established International Criminal Court (ICC). This is clearly because of the precedent set, though before the ICC itself was set up, by the prosecution of the ex-dictator Pinochet, whom the US, and in particular President Nixon's Secretary of State Henry Kissinger, had installed in power.

As NATO has transformed itself from a defensive military alliance of western countries with free market economies into, apparently, a sort of crusading force dedicated to peace and freedom, many have begun to question the assumptions upon which all of this is based. It is tempting to take the view that, far from being designed to preserve or extend peace and the acceptance of humanitarian values, NATO is perhaps rather a sort of military equivalent of the WTO or IMF. This would, in a sense, be a new world order, though beneath the surface it would reveal itself, surely, to be no more than an institutionalised version of the oldest order of all, that of might makes right.

Notes

1. 'A World of Extremes,' *Los Angeles Times*, 17 July 2001
2. *New Internationalist*, Issue 296, online at < http://www.newint.org/issue296/facts.html >
3. *New Internationalist*, Issue 296, online at < http://www.newint.org/issue296/facts.html >
4. Eric Kolodner, *Transnational Corporations: Impediments or Catalysts of Social Development?*, United Nations Research Institute for Social Development, Occasional Paper No. 5, World Summit for Social Development, < http://www.unrisd.org/engindex/publ/list/op/op5/toc.htm >

Conclusion

'…although I can make a lot of suggestions, the point is it's not up to me to provide solutions, it's up to the people concerned. Their solutions will be diverse because of the diversity of their cultures, and will depend on the problems they face, where they face them and so on. Just one example: in a predominantly Muslim community in India, the people were asked what they wanted. Did they need piped water, street lighting…what? And they said, no, we want a mosque. The development agency thought that was clearly the wrong answer, because it was a cultural, spiritual answer. But it turned out that a mosque really was what they needed because they had no place to meet, to have discussions and develop a sense of community.'

Susan George [1]

A Brazilian who was about to move from Milan to Madrid scores a goal seen by hundreds of millions around the world, a moment of superhuman artistry which it is a privilege to share; a Malian musician takes the stage in a concert hall in New York City in a concert to raise money for the victims of an earthquake in India; a German businessman sitting in a hotel room in Guatamala remembers that it is his daughter's birthday: he sets up his laptop, sends her an email, orders her flowers, then goes down to the restaurant to eat. After his meal – lobster from California, asparagus flown up from Argentina, his favourite Australian ice cream, decaffeinated coffee from Jamaica, a fine Chilean wine – he calls her to see if the flowers have arrived and to check that she's read his email. This is globalisation.

But what of the ten-year-old who sowed the ball with which the Brazilian scored his goal, made it by hand in a basement in Karachi? What of him? His parents know he should be at school, but without his meagre earnings they cannot feed their baby or buy her medication, drugs made more expensive than they need be by the self-interest of the pharmaceutical giant which owns the patent. What of the Puerto Rican woman who sweeps the stage when the musicians and their fans have left, who falls asleep on the subway as she hurries home to catch some sleep before rising again at five thirty to get to one of the other two jobs she does to make ends meet? What of the Kenyan farmers who were displaced so that Europeans could receive flowers from their loved ones in the depths of winter?

The rich, the talented and the lucky can treat the world as if it were a village, follow opportunities to earn more money than others might see from a lifetime's toil. The hopeful follow them, joining the flood of the desperate, the determined, the ambitious and the many who have no choice. And the hopeless remain, living and dying in overcrowded cities or the devastated countryside, their always hard lives made harder by processes over which they have no control, dictates signed by faceless men in faraway countries.

This too is globalisation.

11 September 2001, New York City: On a date which needs no explanation, terrorists hijack four aeroplanes. Two are crashed into the twin towers of the World Trade Center. One careers into the Pentagon. Only one is diverted from its target. The mighty engine of globalisation hiccups and proceeds: American leaders deny that their global policies in any sense provoked these events, and no one, or at least no one outside their own country, believes them, or believes even that they believe their own words. America's trade secretary Robert Zoellick says that the answer to terrorism is more trade liberalisation. But the immediate answer is war, a war which, according to Zoellick's defence secretary colleague Donald Rumsfeld, could last for forty years. Globalisation now comes to the bewildered, innocent people of Afghanistan not with the appearance of Coca-Cola signs or golden arches in Kabul, but in a rain of fire, mutilation and death.

Those who argue that globalisation is inevitable, inexorable, and that we should therefore make the most of it, have a problem. As I hope I have demonstrated, specific decisions taken by powerful people, most of them empowered by wealth rather than any democratic process, are what is driving globalisation. People wrote, signed, enacted the treaties and agreements that established the WTO, NAFTA, the European Union. People decide under what conditions the IMF will bail out an economy, what projects the World Bank will back, which countries NATO or the US will bomb or against which the UN will impose sanctions. These people are not driven by some mysterious force outside themselves, and if they wanted to take different decisions they could. For good reasons or bad, they want to see globalisation happen, and this is a major factor motivating their behaviour.

Those who argue that globalisation is beneficial to anyone but a minority of the world's population also have a problem. Inequality, poverty and social exclusion are growing at the same time as the world's GDP continues to mount. In fact, it seems to be precisely when GDP grows that inequality is most likely to widen, a phenomenon which during the 1990s afflicted societies as very different as The Netherlands, Ireland and China.

A factor in the growth of poverty and inequality is the undermining of welfare states, which can be attributed directly to the political economy which accompanies globalisation. The IMF invariably makes cuts in spending on such programmes a condition of its Structural Adjustment Programmes. These mainly affect poorer countries, but the criteria for participation in the EU's Economic and Monetary Union, and its single currency, the Euro, themselves add up to a SAP. Limits on public spending and deficit financing, coupled with pressures to maintain high spending on defence and keep taxes as low as possible (also aspects of globalisation), mean that the welfare state is almost invariably the prime target for cuts. In addition, pressure is mounting to liberalise services and open them to international competition. This in practice means that those aspects of the welfare state which might be potentially profitable – especially healthcare – are being targeted by TNCs looking for new investment opportunities.

It is under such international pressure that the state is retreating from more and more sectors of the economy in more and more countries. At the same time, national governments are increasingly handing over powers to international bodies under no, or at best weak, democratic control. The Treaty which established the European Central Bank (ECB) forbids anyone, including elected political leaders, from interfering in its decisions. This is meant to preserve the Bank's 'independence,' an interesting choice of word. 'Independence' is something we tend to value as individuals and as societies – it is a 'feel-good' word. Yet by this definition, the most independent of all people are dictators and autocrats.

This abdication by the state of numerous responsibilities has lessened the ability of elected politicians to take effective decisions in relation to many of the things that matter most to people. The results, throughout most of the world, are falling turnouts in elections. We cannot elect the real decision-makers, the Chief Executive Officers of major corporations, the heads of the IMF or WTO, the men and women of the European Commission and Central Bank – so why bother? Dramatically falling participation in elections in the UK and US has often been explained by reference to the narrowing of political debate, so that there seems little difference in practice between the various 'brands' on offer. This is no doubt a factor, yet in the first round of the recent French Presidential elections, with two fascists, several centre-right candidates, the social democratic prime minister, an ultra-Thatcherite, a Communist, three Trotskyists and numerous others on offer, there was surely something to suit all tastes. Nevertheless, well over a third of those eligible chose not to vote, and this in what has always been one of Europe's most politicised societies. The only conclusion must be that people felt simply that voting could no longer make much difference, whoever won.

This is also shown by the growing mobile circus of protest which now pursues the great and the good around the globe, appearing, sometimes in hundreds of thousands, outside meetings of heads of government, corporate leaders and international financial and commercial institutions. The destruction of authoritarian systems in Central and Eastern Europe showed what was possible, and that if voting could no longer lead to meaningful change, then taking control of the streets perhaps could. Twenty-five years ago the idea that demonstrations were ineffective was widespread. As a refrain, it now seems as dated as Little Jimmy Osmond singing 'I'm your long haired lover from Liverpool.'

If this is the world that the globalisers want, or are prepared to tolerate, then there is no need for them to concern themselves with the undermining of democracy. They can meet in ever more remote locations, on top of mountains, perhaps, or in the underground bunkers to which the Bush administration famously prepared its retreat after the terrorist attacks on New York and Washington. Perhaps they could create a purpose-built Global Conference Centre on a luxury liner anchored mid-Pacific, or in a geodome at the South Pole. Ideally, they could add an annex to the International Space Station and meet there – though the anti-globalisation movement is so creative that someone would probably learn to fly and build a rocket, just to buzz them. Or they can simply hire more and more police, equip them with more and more sophisticated crowd control weapons, and continue to slug it out.

Alternatively, ways could be found to empower communities, re-empower governments and bring international financial and commercial institutions under some degree of effective popular control. International agreements could ensure that poverty alleviation, human dignity, environmental considerations, public health and the sustainable and equitable use of resources took precedence over short-term and private gain. The fact that trade is a major generator of wealth and contributes to the richness of our lives, and thus the right to trade under as fair a set of rules as possible, should also be recognised and embodied in treaties and permanent institutions, but it should not be raised to a level where it takes precedence over the health of our planet and its inhabitants. A beginning could be made by restructuring taxation so that it bears most heavily on activities which offer private gain at public and environmental cost. The Tobin Tax, discussed in Chapter 5, would be a good starting point.

Admittedly, it is not easy to see how we can get from here to there, at least as long as the United States, by far the world's most powerful nation, plays such a destructive role on the global stage. When the leading industrial power refuses to endorse treaties agreed to by almost every other country – the Kyoto Protocol to the UN agreement on climate change, for example, or the Biodiversity Treaty, or the agreement to make biological weapons illegal – we clearly have a major problem. Yet the fact that the rest of the world wants to proceed by means of negotiation and agreement is encouraging, and we should not allow the limitations of the compromises on which such agreement is necessarily based to disguise that fact. We are at the beginning of a process which might some day give meaning to the relatively newly-coined, but already hackneyed expression, the 'international community.' Unless we are to retreat into the fantasy world of nationalism promoted by the likes of Jean-Marie Le Pen or by the right wing of the British Conservative Party, this is surely the way in which we must respond to globalisation.

'Think globally, act locally,' goes the slogan: so we must begin by giving communities real power over their own lives. From there, we need to resist the erosion of the powers of elected governments, not so that they can build walls around their societies and economies, but to enable states to take meaningful international actions which truly reflect the will of the world's peoples. Another world is indeed possible, but only if we want it, dream of it and work for it.

Note

1. Susan George interviewed in *New Scientist*, 27 April 2002

Reference Materials

Introduction: Global Moments

Mark Weisbrot, *Globalization: A Primer*, available for downloading free of charge from the US Center for Economic and Policy Research Website at < http://www.cepr.net/GlobalPrimer.htm >

New Internationalist, special globalisation edition, < www.newint.org >

Bob Sutcliffe, *100 Ways Of Seeing An Unequal World*, (Zed Books, 2001)

UK Government White Paper, *Making Globalisation Work For The Poor*, < http://www.globalisation.gov.uk/ >

Thomas L. Friedman, *The Lexus And The Olive Tree*, more information about which (including excerpts) can be found at < http://www.lexusandtheolive-tree.com/ >

The Zapatista Rebellion: See the Zapatista Index at < http://flag.blackened.net/revolt/zapatista.html >

NAFTA: US pressure group Public Citizen's appraisal < http://www.citizen.org/pctrade/nafta/naftapg.html >

Seattle: Links to all points of view < http://www.globalissues.org/TradeRelated/Seattle.asp >

Globalising football: Steve Greenfield and Guy Osborn, *Regulating Football: Commodification, Consumption And The Law* (London: Pluto Press, 2001)

World Music: Links to hundreds of sites < http://www.worldmusicportal.com/ >

1: Definitions

The most comprehensive discussion of definitions of globalisation, and one of the best sources of information on the subject, is at < http://globalization.about.com/ >

2: Globalisation Then And Now

A Quick Guide to the World History of Globalization < http://www.sas.upenn.edu/~dludden/global1.htm > Follow the links for a variety of material.

3: Winners And Losers

United Nations' Development Project *Budgets As If People Mattered* (UNDP, 2000) available at < http://www.undp.org/ >

Tore Linné Eriksen 'Globalization: Winners And Losers' at < http://www.u-fon-det.no/artikler/globalTLEeng.htm >

'Why GDP Is An Inappropriate Measure Of Economic Health,' brief explanation with links to more detailed analyses at < http://www.globalexchange.org/economy/econ101/gdp.html >

4: Managing Globalisation

Danial Altman, 'As Global Lenders Refocus, A Needy World Waits,' *New York Times*, 3 February 2002, < http://www.nytimes.com/2002/03/17/business/yourmoney/17BANK.html >

WTO official Website < www.wto.org >

WTO critical Website < www.wtowatch.org >

IMF official Website < www.imf.org >

World Bank official Website < www.worldbank.org >

IMF/World Bank critical websites < www.globalexchange.org > and < http://www.50years.org/ >

Official NATO websites < www.nato.int > and < www.natonews.com >

Official EU Website portal, leading to all institutions < www.europa.int >

Steven P. McGiffen, *The European Union: A Critical Guide* (Pluto Press, 2002)

5: Globalise This!

Edward S. Herman and Robert W. McChesney, *The Global Media: The New Missionaries Of Global Capitalism* (Cassell, 1997)

Anti-globalisation Website < www.users.bigpond.com >

Canadian intelligence service report on anti-globalisation movements < http://www.csis-scrs.gc.ca/eng/miscdocs/200008_e.html >

A wide range of links < http://internet.ggu.edu/university_library/if/ftaa.html >

World Social Forum < www.forumsocialmundial.org.br >

ATTAC < http://www.attac.org/indexfla.htm >

Via Campesina < http://ns.rds.org.hn/via/english.htm >

Indymedia, links to all affiliates sites < www.indymedia.org >

Schnews < www.schnews.org.uk >

Corpwatch < www.corpwatch.org >

Spectre < www.spectrezine.org >

World Socialist Website < www.wsws.org >

See also < www.commondreams.org >

6: Battlefields

Debt

UNICEF < www.unicef.org >

COCAD, campaigns for relief or Third World Debt < http://users.skynet.be/cadtm/pages/english/english.htm >

Jubilee 2000, ditto < www.jubilee2000uk.org >

Eric Toussaint, *Your Money Or Your Life* (Pluto Press, 1998)

Food

United Nations Food and Agriculture Organisation < www.fao.org >

Global campaign for agrarian reform < www.foodfirst.org >

Jonathan King and Doreen Stabinsky, 'Biotechnology Under Globalisation: The Corporate Expropriation Of Plant, Animal And Microbial Species,' *Race And Class* 40, January 1999

Work

Eric Kolodner, *Transnational Corporations: Impediments Or Catalysts Of Social Development?* United Nations Research Institute for Social Development, Occasional Paper No. 5, World Summit for Social Development < http://www.unrisd.org/engindex/publ/list/op/op5/toc.htm >

War

Hamdi A. Hassan, *The Iraqi Invasion Of Kuwait* (Pluto Press, 1999)

Voices in the Wilderness, campaign to end sanctions against the people of Iraq < http://www.nonviolence.org/vitw/ >

Jeane J. Kirkpatrick, 'Why Are We in Kosovo?' < www.aei.org >

Peter Gowan, *The Twisted Road To Kosovo* (Oxford: Labour Focus on Eastern Europe No 62, Special Edition)

'The US/NATO War in Yugoslavia: Eight Myths,' < http://www.iacenter.org/myths.htm >

Official US view of the bombing campaign in Afghanistan, its causes and aftermath < http://usgovinfo.about.com >

Critical views and reports on same at < http://www.intercircle.net/ >

General

George Soros, *George Soros On Globalization* (Perseus Books Public Affairs, 2002)

Tariq Ali, *The Clash Of Fundamentalisms: Crusades, Jihad And Modernity* (Verso, 2002)

Wim Dierckxsens, *The Limits Of Capitalism: An Approach To Globalization Without Neoliberalism* (Zed Books, 2001)

Susan George, *The Lugano Report* (Pluto Press, 2001)

Finally, follow the host of links to all shades of opinion at the excellent Website *Globalization Issues* < http://globalization.about.com/ >

The Essential Library: Currently Available

Film Directors:

Woody Allen (2nd)	Tim Burton	Ang Lee
Jane Campion*	John Carpenter	Joel & Ethan Coen (2nd)
Jackie Chan	Steven Soderbergh	Clint Eastwood
David Cronenberg	Terry Gilliam*	Michael Mann
Alfred Hitchcock (2nd)	Krzysztof Kieslowski*	Roman Polanski
Stanley Kubrick (2nd)	Sergio Leone	Oliver Stone
David Lynch	Brian De Palma*	George Lucas
Sam Peckinpah*	Ridley Scott (2nd)	James Cameron
Orson Welles (2nd)	Billy Wilder	
Steven Spielberg	Mike Hodges	

Film Genres:

Blaxploitation Films	Bollywood	French New Wave
Horror Films	Spaghetti Westerns	Vietnam War Movies
Slasher Movies	Film Noir	Hammer Films
Vampire Films*	Heroic Bloodshed*	Carry On Films
German Expressionist Films		

Film Subjects:

Laurel & Hardy	Marx Brothers	Film Music
Steve McQueen*	Marilyn Monroe	The Oscars® (2nd)
Filming On A Microbudget	Bruce Lee	Writing A Screenplay
Film Studies		

Music:

The Madchester Scene	Beastie Boys	Jethro Tull
How To Succeed In The Music Business		

Literature:

Cyberpunk	Philip K Dick	The Beat Generation
Agatha Christie	Sherlock Holmes	Noir Fiction*
Terry Pratchett	Hitchhiker's Guide (2nd)	Alan Moore
William Shakespeare	Creative Writing	Tintin

Ideas:

Conspiracy Theories	Nietzsche	UFOs
Feminism	Freud & Psychoanalysis	Bisexuality

History:

Alchemy & Alchemists	The Crusades	The Black Death
Jack The Ripper	The Rise Of New Labour	Ancient Greece
American Civil War	American Indian Wars	Witchcraft
Globalisation	Who Shot JFK?	

Miscellaneous:

Stock Market Essentials	How To Succeed As A Sports Agent	Doctor Who

Available at bookstores or send a cheque (payable to 'Oldcastle Books') to: **Pocket Essentials (Dept G), P O Box 394, Harpenden, Herts, AL5 1XJ, UK**. £3.99 each (£2.99 if marked with an *). For each book add 50p(UK)/£1 (elsewhere) postage & packing